OPINION ESSAYS

FOR SEASONED CITIZENS

AND THEIR ELDERS

By

Walt Sonneville

Copyright 2013
Walt Sonneville

Waltson Publishing Co.
314 Wye Mill Court
Gaithersburg, MD 20879
301 869 4460

TABLE OF CONTENTS

Essay	Title	Page
i	Introduction	
1	Infatuation at First Sight	1
2	Our Bequeath to Future Generations	7
3	Changing Fashions in Our Daily Bread	11
4	Care-givers in the Home Infirmary	17
5	Senior-Citizen Laureates	23
6	Good Looks and Looking Good	29
7	Recalling Past Events	35
8	Withering Pensions and Encore Careers	39
9	Enhancing Our Hearing	45
10	Chivalry is Not Entirely Dead	51
11	Our Fading Away	57
12	Will Sartorial Splendor Return	63
13	The Gender-War Armistice	69
14	Reconsidering Our National Motto	75
15	Trust, but Verify	79
16	Mind Your Manners	83
17	Swearing	89
18	Miracles and Wonders	95
19	Our Divisible Nation	99
20	Achieving the American Dream	103
21	First Ladies as Associate Presidents	109
22	Proposed: A Council of Sages	115

Essay	Title	Page
23	Bathing: Now and Then	121
24	Each of us is a Time Capsule	127
25	Dogs, Children or Neither	131
26	Lies—White and Other	137
27	Silver Linings on our Aging Shadow	145
28	Talk, Talk, Talk	149
29	Why Good Things Happen to Evil People	153
30	Driving While Aged	157
31	The Rise of Our Women Warriors	165
32	Is Everybody Happy	173
33	Don't Expect This to Happen	181

INTRODUCTION

This book completes a trilogy of personal-opinion essays. Its two companion books, published earlier, are: <u>My 22 Cents Worth</u> and <u>A Musing Moment</u>. The title of this book, <u>Opinion Essays for Seasoned Citizens and Their Elders</u>, reflects the intended reading audience for all three books.

"Seasoned Citizens" are mature adults—not necessarily senior citizens, but assuredly experienced—who re-examine impressions from the annals of their personal book of life. The "Elders" often are seasoned as well, but likely to be a generation or two older and endowed with more chapters in their annals.

More books should be written by and for the seasoned and their elders. Harold Ickes, our longest-serving cabinet member (1933-1946), lamented: "I have often wished that my father and his father … had left some written record, however brief, of their lives and times. To most of us … our ancestors are only names." Ickes followed his own advice by writing, at the age of 69, <u>The Autobiography of a Curmudgeon</u> (1943), providing a record of his life, times and, most importantly, his impressions.

One never is too old to write. If you have not written for your descendents, take encouragement from the examples of book authors Herman Wouk, Martha Ann Miller, and Diana Athill. Mr. Wouk, the celebrated author of <u>The Caine Mutiny</u>, published in 1951, has written a 234-page novel, entitled <u>The Lawgiver</u>, which was released in 2012 when he was 97 years old. Ms. Miller, of Arlington County, Virginia, at the age of 100 had her 255-page autobiography published, also in 2012. British writer Athill was a category winner of the Costa Book Awards for her memoir entitled <u>Somewhere Towards the End</u>, published in 2008 when she reached 92 years of age.

Our own lives, times and impressions could be sufficiently revealed in essay form. Writing an essay is less challenging than writing a book, and more likely to be read. Essays are almost always short, typically up to 2,000 words (about twice as long as this Introduction). The paragraphs are not long, a constraint that was ignored by Ralph Waldo Emerson, America's first great essayist, when he wrote the best-known of his many essays, "The American Scholar" (1837).

The essay genre is an ideal literary form to ruminate on the bits and pieces of life: our looks, infatuations, clothing, manners, pets, happiness and much more. Let us leave the preeminent issues of life—health, faith, and income—to medical professionals, philosophers, financial advisors and the clergy. There is an abundance of such essays.

The essay format covers a complex of sub-genres. They include, among others: fiction, non-fiction, opinion, memoir, historic, humor, travel, philosophical, and critique.

Essays are superb for anthologies of related topics. They allow the reader to pick and choose according to the topic of interest and the appeal of the writer's style. Topics should avoid dependency on current news, which is the distinguishing feature of journalism.

Good essays have no expiration date. John Locke, Francis Bacon, Samuel Johnson, G. K. Chesterton and Michel Eyquem de Montaigne (1533-1592), the renaissance writer who inspired the genre and gave it the name "essay," continue to interest modern readers with their classic, timeless essays.

Few writers choose essay writing as their primary vocation. Normally, it is an avocation. Writers come from many backgrounds, as shown by famous essayists recognized for accomplishments other than writing essays. They include

Einstein, Orwell, Faulkner, Lincoln, Franklin, Mencken, Poe, Vidal, Updike, and Martin Luther King.

Mark Twain, renowned for two classic novels, ranks equally high as an essayist. Wendell Berry, a popular modern essayist, is a farmer. Many well-known poets were essayists (e.g., T.S. Eliot, Walt Whitman, and Ezra Pound).

Publishers do not want to see the word "essay" in book titles. They prefer to market their offerings so they appear distinct from the essay form commonly tasked to us as students. Consequently, the word "essay" has led to selection of several alternative nouns. Its definition is convoluted in a flotsam of synonyms: articles, columns, monographs, reviews, polemics, discourses—and the archaic alternatives called compositions and themes.

Irwin Edman wrote, in his introduction to <u>Emerson's Essays</u> (1951): "the essay has almost vanished from the world of modern writing." He is mistaken. The *word* has almost vanished but essays remain with us under different banners, as Wilfrid Sheed indicates in his book <u>Essays in Disguise</u> (1990).

Montaigne, a French aristocrat, used the word *essai* as a verb, as in *faire l'essai de* (to try out or attempt or test). His purpose was to test or judge his philosophical perspectives and cultural opinions by exploring them anew in the process of writing an essay. He expected his writings would be of interest to a few readers for a short time. The Vatican worked to impose this expectation by placing his book, *Essais*, on their Index of Prohibited Books, from 1676 to 1854.

That prohibition may have elevated Montaigne's literary influence, just as books deemed "morally objectionable" increased public interest once Boston banned their public distribution. The city abandoned its "Banned-in-Boston" practice in 1965, acknowledging it was counter-productive. Some of America's greatest and most-popular fiction writers found the ban added significantly to their market appeal elsewhere. An essayist could only hope for such good fortune.

This book of 33 essays explores topics that are more mundane than philosophical or esoteric. The essays look at bits and pieces of life in which we have our own personal impressions and opinions.

Walt Sonneville

1
INFATUATION AT FIRST SIGHT

In both folklore and literature there is the phenomenon of "love at first sight." It happens to some people. Marc Antony and Cleopatra, Romeo and Juliet, Napoleon and Josephine are prominent examples. They had to fall in love at first sight. There was no time to waste. Bad things caught up quickly with these couples.

Christopher Marlowe (1564-1593), poet and playwright, coined this couplet to defend the reality of love at first sight: "Where both deliberate, the love is slight. Who ever loved, that loved not at first sight?" Shakespeare liked the lines so well he virtually copied them for one of his plays.

In folklore we find many examples. Children may believe their parents fell in love at first sight. But when mama is asked for details she may demur, noting: "Well, it didn't quite happen that way."

According to *Newsweek* Magazine (2-13-12), 34% of men and 27% of women say they have experienced love at first sight. These percentages seem surprisingly low. Perhaps those who did not admit to such an experience banished the memory. Some of us have fallen in love at first sight more than once.

How often do we hear of people falling in love at first sight in their senior years? Not often. The sensation is reserved almost entirely for the vulnerable young, those who experience almost-instant hormonal arousal, an adrenaline rush, a sweaty palpitation or a fear-of-failure introduction where words stumble out awkwardly. The sensation is real, but the affection is bogus.

When we read of older people falling in love at first sight, it is frequently an aged man falling for a woman young enough to be his grand-daughter. These cases are newsworthy because they are rare. Oil tycoon J. Howard Marshall was 89 when he married 26-year-old Anna Nicole Smith. Their marriage lasted 14 months, at which time he expired. Supreme Court Justice William Douglas was 68 when he married Cathleen Heffernan, 22 years of age. That marriage lasted 14 years, at which time he expired. Both couples satisfied their vows of "'till death do us part.'"

How can we tell that it is truly love at first sight? It is apparent in the eyes of the enamored. Several renowned persons have been credited with originating the famous line:

"the eyes are the windows to the soul." It seems everyone wants to claim authorship.

Eyes do reveal feelings, including passion. When one feels a strong attraction towards another, the pupils are said to dilate. This draws more attention to the eyes. Much can be communicated through eye contact. Barry and Greenwich truly had insight when they titled their popular song "The Look of Love is in Your Eyes."

Opposite personalities who discover instinctive attraction to each other represent a more realistic phenomenon than love at first sight. Instinctive attraction at first sight doesn't necessarily indicate interest in a long-term relationship. One may admire in the other those characteristics one lacks, such as sociability, humor, ambition, knowledge, or a musical, dance, or athletic talent. Opposites can introduce each other to new interests. Sameness can be boring. *Viva la difference* is the hallmark bond of many happy partnerships.

Differences have limits in retaining interests. Couples sharing core values, attitudes and religions have a more durable bonding than those who lack such commonalities. This is the conclusion reached by researchers at the University of Iowa (*Journal of Personality and Social*

Psychology, February 2005). Our routine untrained observations confirm what those professional researchers laboriously concluded.

Some differences are implanted in the relationship from the beginning. Men and women are psychologically different. John Gray elaborated this point in his <u>Men are From Mars, Women are from Venus</u>, a book that sold over 7 million copies. Isn't this something we learned in our teens?

In a satisfying continuing relationship, our differences are complementary. She is naturally submissive, while he is moderately domineering. Or, he is shy while she is an extrovert. Somehow a workable balance is reached.

In young people the reproductive genetic search, either at the conscious or sub-conscious level, drives us to seek a partner with particular features to endow any offspring that might issue. It could be an attraction to nice hair, white teeth, small ears, high cheek bones, long eye lashes—features that offset deficiencies we feel about ourselves.

As we age into our senior years, we become less attracted by physical features. We look for similarities that enhance companionship. We appreciate the importance of differences in our schedules so we have some privacy to read, meditate, listen to music or view television in pursuit of our own interests.

An enduring relationship requires a measure of humility by both partners.   One should yield on occasion in the expectation of prevailing some other time.   That helps preserve love until the last sight.

2

OUR BEQUEATH TO FUTURE GENERATIONS

What would you like to see today's youngest generation bequeath to future generations? More time to enjoy life and less time for work? A single language adopted by all nations? Cures for diseases? These and other hopes turn frail if there is no sustainable environment to bequeath. Mother Earth needs our support if future generations are to enjoy her bounty.

The Confederation of the Six Nations of the Iroquois adopted a constitution, called the "Great Binding Law," that required each nation to protect the generations to come when reaching tribal decisions, particularly environmental decisions. The Council of the Confederation was directed by the document's language to "look and listen for the welfare of the whole people and have always in view not only the present, but also the coming generations." Their constitution predates, by several centuries, the year 1772 when the sixth Iroquois nation joined the confederacy.

The U.S. Constitution, adopted in 1787, does not speak specifically of protecting the environment of future generations. It begins by mentioning why our constitution was adopted, reading in part to "promote the general welfare, and secure the blessings of liberty to ourselves and our posterity…"

It is difficult to secure blessings to future generations if the environment is left in ruins. A study conducted by the Harvard Law School, "Models for Protecting the Environment for Future Generations" (October 2008), identified three state constitutions (Hawaii, Illinois, and Montana), and five state statutes that reference "the protection of the environment for future as well as present generations." The study adds that at least eight U.S. federal statutes make a similar reference.

Responsibility to ensure environmental protection for the needs of future generations was adopted in 1972 by signatories to the "Stockholm Declaration on the Human Environment" of the United Nations Conference on the Human Environment. In 1997 the same responsibility was urged upon nations by the U.N. Educational, Scientific, and Cultural Organization when it adopted its "Declaration on the Responsibilities for the Present Generations toward Future Generations."

In the early 1990s, famed sea-explorer Jacques Cousteau began a petition for a Bill of Rights for Future Generations in which "every person has the right to inherit an uncontaminated planet on which all forms of life may flourish." Nine million people signed the petition, which was submitted on October 17, 2001 to the Secretary General of the United Nations, Mr. Kofi Annan.

Protection of our environment is an issue endorsed today by almost all Americans. This value extends over many past decades by some of our presidents. Lincoln protected California's Yosemite Valley by setting aside land that later became a national park. President Theodore Roosevelt went much further by protecting 230 million acres as national forests, wildlife refuges, parks and preserves.

To borrow a phrase, the road to environmental doom is paved with good intentions. In the past century our population more than tripled from 92 million to 320 million. The U.S. Department of Agriculture reported, in its 2007 National Resources Inventory: "Annually, we now lose about 1.6 million acres of working farms, ranches, and forests to fragmentation and development. Many of our rivers, lakes, coasts, and streams are polluted. Fish advisories and beach closures occur frequently."

We might add more details to this list of assaults on the environment: mountain-top removal to mine coal, poorly-conceived damming of rivers and irrigation, ocean waters turning acidic, poorly-secured nuclear waste, the infestation of invasive plants and fish, ozone depletion, and the battle between resource-removal employment and a sustainable environment.

Each generation inherits life. It should follow that each generation also inherits temporary custody of the life-giving resources of the planet. As sojourners on earth we are temporary stewards of its resources, obligated to protect them for the sustenance of ourselves, our children and their descendants.

Albert Camus, the French philosopher and novelist, offered this observation in his 1946 essay, "The Crisis of Man": "I do not believe in guaranteed progress, or in any philosophy of history, but I think that, at least, man has never ceased to advance in the awareness of our destiny. We have not overcome our conditions, but at least we understand them better." At the moment, it seems awareness and overcoming have yet to make their mutual acquaintance.

3

CHANGING FASHIONS IN OUR DAILY BREAD

Food changes come into fashion and then fade. Until about 1955 lard (pork fat) was the preferred ingredient for a good pie crust and for frying. Then we switched to vegetable shortening or oil blends, the healthful benefits of which are questioned today because of their partially-hydrogenated content.

By 1957 consumption of margarine (a product of vegetable oil) exceeded butter for the first time. Our potatoes then, but less so today, were accompanied with plenty of gravy, if not margarine, sour cream, an au-gratin topping or "scalloped" layers of butter, milk and cheese. Peas could be served creamed and spinach, asparagus or corn might be baked into a fluffy, fat-laden soufflé.

Meat dishes included pot roast, "Swiss" steak, fried chicken, liver and onions, and large links of sausage. If we were in too much of a rush to prepare these meats, a canned loaf of processed ham ("Spam") might be the main entrée. Cow tongue or calf brains were familiar selections. Ox-tail and turtles made tasty soups.

Our daily bread was served without guilt. Moments of gastronomical indulgence, we felt, were well deserved, especially for those whose workday involved manual labor. Meals were a sensual excursion in which we delighted our taste memories.

Food choices were associated with preferred states of origin. The better potatoes came from Idaho, cherries from Michigan, apples from Washington, cheese from Wisconsin, and country ham from Virginia. Today we are encouraged to "buy local" to reduce transportation costs. Buying local is a formidable challenge when tempted by the lower prices of imported products or availability from a region that enjoys a flavor-enhancing climate.

Food fashions change. The U.S. Department of Agriculture reports that annual meat consumption per person fell from 184 pounds to 171 pounds (the boneless equivalent) during the period 2004 to 2011. Consumption of beef has fallen from 91 pounds per capita in 1976 (the peak year) to an estimated 52 pounds in 2012. Since 1990 Americans have been eating more chicken than beef. Pork consumption reached its peak in 1944 at 54 pounds per person, falling to an estimated 44 pounds in 2012.

Beginning in the early 1990s, we began consuming meat-styled soy products. Appearance counts. It must look like meat even if the taste is vaguely comparable. As corn prices rose in 2012 to $7.50 a bushel—thanks to the demand for corn ethanol—the rising cost of animal feed threatens to make real meat a mere memory.

Seafood has become a popular alternative to meat. Fish-processing boats, called "factory boats," are rapidly depleting the remaining stock of fish in the wild, raising the prospect that soy, or perhaps seaweed-based "seafood," may become an alternative choice in the coming decade.

Today the preference for food selections frequently is driven by their perceived nutrient content, rather than taste. Whole grains rich in fiber, fat-free, gluten-free, and calories per serving are factors that increasingly decide our choices.

Our vocabulary has expanded to evaluate how choices are made. Anti-oxidants, amino acids, omega-3 fatty acids, trans-fat, free-radicals, triglycerides, monounsaturated, polyunsaturated, and probiotics are some of the words we struggle to interpret. It's enough to slacken one's appetite.

As women became increasingly employed we ate more meals out, poorly informed to the health consequences. The U.S. Department of Agriculture states that "eating out has been popular for Americans over the past several decades. In 1970 26% of all food spending was on food away from home. By 2005 (latest data) that share rose to 41 percent." The department then notes that food prepared away from home contains more calories and fewer nutrients "per eating occasion" than at-home foods. Their study indicated a "positive association" between eating out and obesity. Since 1980 Americans have added an average of 300 calories daily per person.

Is our craving for pizza a principal cause of our higher caloric consumption? Pizza in our country has been available since first introduced in New York City in 1902. It wasn't until the early 1950s, however, that it began to be widely available. Its popularity has surged since.

Don't overlook the transition from the by-gone cafeterias, where we paid a-la-carte before these facilities were replaced by "all-you-can" eat fixed-prize buffet restaurants. Gourmand-themed establishments should alter their promotion to "all-you-care to eat," suggesting that modesty in our consumption helps avoid more than just gastric penalties.

Eating has turned from a pleasure to a sometimes risky adventure. We enjoy the taste while on guard not only for carcinogens, but for e-coli and salmonella alerts as well. Consuming too much sugar, dairy products, red meat, artificial sweeteners, and carbohydrates are concerns that cast ominous shadows over our meal plates.

One culinary joy that has remained innocent in our perception of healthful foods is a peanut-butter-and-jelly sandwich. It has been popular since the 1920s. We give thanks for our daily bread, especially when it is spread with "PB&J."

4

CARE-GIVERS IN THE HOME INFIRMARY

When the elderly become ill, frail, or disabled, home usually is their first choice as the repose sanctuary. If that entails care given by an employed relative, the choice is compromised by loss of income. If given by a person with insufficient energy, fatigue sets boundaries on the care given.

For those faced with such limitations, there has to be hope for a better way. With all of the proposed and tried health-care programs nationally, we should expect at least one program for care-giving to emerge as having the potential to succeed.

There appears to be such a model. It is called the "Program of All-Inclusive Care for the Elderly" (PACE). Before discussing the features of PACE, let's examine the rationale for why a care-giver program needs to be considered for availability nationwide.

The "problem" is our aging demographics. Growth in the number of elderly Americans, 65 years of age or more, brings unwieldy pressure on the capabilities of the nation's health-care delivery system as presently constituted. The number of Baby Boomers (those born between 1946 and 1964) who are 65 years or older will double from 35 million in the year 2001 to 71 million by 2030, significantly outpacing the 33% growth in the nation's total population in those three decades.

The average length of stay in a nursing home is 835 days, according to the Center for Disease Control and Prevention. The median cost per year nationally is $74,000. *The New York Times* reported (2-23-12) that "nursing homes, which tend to rely heavily on Medicare and Medicaid dollars, are facing enormous financial pressure. Nationally, the number of nursing homes has declined by nearly 350 in the past six years." The Kaiser Foundation reports there were 15,622 nursing homes in the United States in 2010.

Caring for the 6 million elderly, who currently need home health-care assistance, is borne mostly by those remarkable troopers we call "domestic care-givers." There are approximately 10 million unpaid care-givers in this nation who provide long-term home care to senior citizens. They are the spouses, siblings, children, partners, grandchildren and friends who provide an estimated 80% of the time dedicated to elderly care.

Initially daunted by the responsibility, many domestic care-givers discover a sense of emotional satisfaction as the responsibility proceeds. That satisfaction is scaled, depending on the amount of stress from unrelieved assistance, financial hardship, and neglect to their own health caused by anxiety and fatigue.

As marriages take place later in life, middle-aged couples can find themselves "sandwiched" between taking care of their minor children and assisting in the care of an elderly parent. AARP reports that 40% of its members provide financial support for their parents *and* children.

PACE day-care centers provide relief to domestic care-givers. They allow employed care-givers to continue to earn an income by arranging relief at the centers during day-time hours. Those given care enjoy the familiarity and comforts of staying home during the night.

PACE Centers are non-profit organizations funded as a component of Medicare and, in those states opting to support it, Medicaid. They serve as an economical alternative to nursing homes.

The centers provide nursing, physical, occupational and recreational therapies, meals, prescription drugs and medical care. Financing is capped per individual, allowing providers to deliver to participants any of their various needs rather than billing on a per-service basis.

PACE currently is available in only 30 states and not in all regions of those states. Pennsylvania has the most PACE Centers (17) and New York the second most (9).

PACE was inspired by a private initiative in California that began in 1971. It wasn't until 1990 that the first PACE Center was given funding waivers under Medicare and Medicaid. By 1996 there were 21 PACE Centers in 15 states, increasing in 2007 to 42 in 22 states and, in 2011, 82 centers in 30 states.

States in which PACE Centers are not available, as of 2011, are: Alaska, Arizona, Connecticut, Delaware, Georgia, Hawaii, Idaho, Indiana, Kentucky, Maine, Minnesota, Missouri, Montana, Nebraska, Nevada, New Hampshire, South Dakota, Utah, West Virginia, and Wyoming.

If these non-profit PACE Centers increase at a rate faster than the states supporting the program, we have implied evidence that PACE appears to be a success. The alternative of for-profit adult day-care centers is forbiddingly expensive to most elderly. It is reported that day-care centers have an average price of about $64 a day per patient, excluding cost of professionally-administrated medical health-care services.

SENIOR-CITIZEN LAUREATES

Seniors deserve special recognition if they have served as remarkable examples of achievement in their elderly years. A title, awarded by a prestigious authority such as state governors or the president, would be fitting. A proposed title is Senior-Citizen Laureate.

An example of recognition for outstanding service is the British Empire Medal for Meritorious Service, commonly called the B.E.M. Although it ranks as the fifth of six levels of UK medals, the B.E.M. nonetheless enjoys a proud status.

Life Magazine (1-29-51) had a feature article on Fanny Thorne, then an 88-year-old great grandmother. She had been awarded the B.E.M. in 1951 by King George VI to honor her for continuing to toil on her farm, six days a week, from the time her husband died in World War I to 1951.

The award was for "her devoted service to agriculture." In 1943, at the age of 80, Mrs. Thorne demonstrated extraordinary stamina when, according to the magazine, she "shucked an eight-acre field of barley by herself in 11 hours and 30 minutes." Her routine tasks included threshing wheat, sorting potatoes, and cutting kale to feed the cattle. She lived alone in her four-room cottage.

This exceptional woman won her medal by going far beyond what might be expected of the human body. Medals should be awarded as well for those who render outstanding, if not Herculean, contributions.

Why not an American medal specifically to recognize seniors who accomplish remarkable achievements in their advanced years? Our country has several types of medals to recognize other exceptional civilians. They include the U.S. Presidential Medal of Freedom, the Congressional Gold Medal, the Presidential Citizens Medal, the National Medal of Arts, and the National Medal of Technology and Innovation.

Young people have two types of medals awarded, both by the U.S. Department of Justice. One is the Young American Medal for Bravery. The other is the Young American Medal for Service. Seniors are deserving of recognition for their services as well.

Older people are increasingly becoming a larger sector of our demographics. This invites criticism from some younger people who view this "silver tsunami" as a strain on government budgets and families of the elderly. Living long lives can lead to intergenerational conflicts, unless counter measures are adopted commending both the outstanding elderly and the young.

To promote intergenerational harmony, seniors able to do so may wish to volunteer for occasional assignments with non-profit organizations, including local and county governments, social and faith-based groups, and service organizations. This would ease the fiscal burdens faced by non-profits and burnish the esteem to which seniors are held.

The U.S. Census Bureau's "Current Populations Survey" found that in 2010 approximately 26.3% of Americans over the age of 16 volunteered. For women the rate was 29.3% and for men it was 23.2 percent.

The rate for men and women combined, ages 55-64, was 27.2%, dropping to 23.6% for those 65 and older. Recognizing Senior-Citizen Laureates could encourage raised levels of participation.

A report by the Urban Institute, entitled "Late Fall 2011 Nonprofit Fundraising Study," states that of the 875 non-profits responding to its survey, 54% are looking for volunteers for administrative work. Another study by the same institute, "Volunteer Transitions among Older Americans" (12-13-07), using 2002 data, found "the time that adults age 55 and older devoted to formal volunteer activities has been valued at $44 billion, and this estimate is likely to increase as the large Baby Boom generation grows older."

What benefit is there to seniors who volunteer? A study published in the journal *Social Science and Medicine* (November 2010) finds that elderly persons who volunteer live longer and healthier. The data are based on a study of 916 non-institutionalized American seniors, ages 65 or older who are "cognitively functional." Volunteering provided them a sense of purpose, the study concluded.

May is the appropriate month to announce the names of perhaps a dozen national honorees selected annually as "Senior Laureates." May is designated as "Older Americans Month," a program originated by the Kennedy administration. It is celebrated across the country through ceremonies and events, and is managed by the Administration on Aging of the Department of Health and Human Services.

The theme for Older Americans Month in 2012 was "Never Too Old to Play!" The theme was selected to encourage older Americans to stay engaged, active and involved in their communities.

Honoring inspirational seniors who are civically engaged could raise the level of volunteerism among older Americans, enhance their sense of purpose, support deserving non-profits, and raise the stature of seniors among their own and younger generations. Laureates, lead the way!

6

GOOD LOOKS AND LOOKING GOOD

In one corner is the undefeated reigning champion, Father Time. In the other corner is the challenger, Our Good Looks. You know how this fight will end. The question is: How many rounds will it last, and which will be the decisive round?

Good Looks have advantages in the first two trimesters of an aged life. When we enter our senior years, looks that may arouse interests from the opposite sex typically have almost entirely vanished. Who cares? By that time our primary objectives are to feel good and look good, forsaking any hope of good looks.

Eleanor Roosevelt was no eye-catching beauty. She recognized the value of our overall appearance this way: "Beautiful young people," she said, "are accidents of nature, but beautiful old people are works of art." Maybe we aren't "works of art" in the classic sense. But if we have a twinkle in our eyes and a smile on our face, we can look good without being good looking.

Once our good looks begin to vanish, we have other resources to display: charm, kindness, knowledge, integrity, humor and, as Eleanor Roosevelt has shown, a measure of wisdom. They are all part of looking good.

There were times Abraham Lincoln depended on self-deprecating humor when campaigning for election. Henry Villard, a journalist who covered the Lincoln-Douglas debates, wrote Lincoln had a "gawky figure, an odd-featured, wrinkled, inexpressive and altogether uncomely face." When Stephan A. Douglas called Lincoln "two-faced," Lincoln replied: "I leave it to the audience. If I had another face, do you think I would wear this one?" This retort scored "Father Abraham," as he was called by those who saw in him a biblical image, election points that otherwise may have been denied him because of his lack of good looks.

Comic Jimmy Durante and Physicist Albert Einstein were not handsome. Yet people found them appealing because their appearance matched the public's image-expectations for the roles each prominently held in life. Their looks were as if each was an actor supplied by a Hollywood studio's department of central casting.

Einstein, despite his brilliance, could not grasp his public popularity. He wondered why "no one understands me but they like me anyway. I don't understand it."

Our faces have to be compatible with the stereotypical image the public has of certain professions. Would Jimmy Durante look credible as a world-renowned scientist and would Albert Einstein find popular support as a comedian? Would a movie entitled "Strange Love Affair" have a chance as a box-office success if it starred "Groucho" Marx and Elizabeth Taylor? Our looks, good or not, support or limit us in our destined roles in life.

Richard Nixon is said to have lost voter appeal in his 1960 televised debate with presidential-candidate Jack Kennedy. It was not due to Nixon's discussion of the issues, which he handled quite well. He lost appeal because of his whisker-stubble, commonly called a "five o'clock shadow" in the jargon of the 1960s. To some, the stubble made him look un-presidential, somewhat malevolent.

Roles in life are determined largely by more than just our bodies. It is our image in its entirety, including our clothing style down to the type of eye glasses we wear. Doesn't a Franciscan monk receive more public reverence when garbed in a brown robe, or a doctor given more credibility when wearing a white medical jacket?   Imagine them both in tee-shirts and jeans.

As we enter our senior years, we should give more attention to an appropriate dress style. It makes us feel better and raises the favorability quotient for how we are perceived by others.

Physical attractiveness need not be limited entirely to the young. Several famed movie stars retained a visage appeal—if not their sex appeal—as they turned elderly. Jimmy Stewart, Cary Grant, Paul Newman, Henry Fonda, Mary Martin, Myrna Loy, Barbara Stanwyck, and Greer Garson are among them. They were graced with the beauty of dignity, experience, and credibility despite their advancing years.

Seniors are past the age when they indulge their vanities in cosmetic makeovers, such as botox injections, breast implants, liposuction and other beautification procedures. These temporary time-reversing treatments typically are for those entering their forties. Undergoing medical cosmetology is not aging gracefully, it is grasping to retain vanishing good looks rather than refining the emerging persona whose focus should be on looking good.

What happens to the body of a man with a muscle-bound torso once he reaches the fifth decade of life and beyond? Based on photos of Arnold Schwarzenegger in swimming trunks, his "Mr. Universe" physique has badly deteriorated. It takes most body-builders two hours a day, six days a week, of weight lifting to look like a modern Goliath.

After the age of 50 we lose about 3% of our lean body mass per decade, most of which is muscle. It takes more time and energy than most of us are able to dedicate to overcome that loss. It is a vainglorious mission.

7

RECALLING PAST EVENTS

Maurice Chevalier's and Hermione Gingold's vocal duet popularized the song "I Remember it Well," written by Lerner and Lowe for the film *Gigi*. Chevalier's character reminisces about how they met. He sings: "We met at nine." She replies: "We met at eight."

The back-and-forth continues. "I was on time." "No, you were late." "Ah yes, I remember it well. We dined with friends." "No, we dined alone." "A tenor sang." "No, a baritone."

"Ah yes, I remember it well."

After correcting his every remembrance, he asks: "Am I getting old?" She lovingly replies: "Oh, no, not you."

The poor fellow has faulty long-term memory. It is short-term memory that bewilders most of us as we age. How often have you wondered why you entered a room to retrieve something? What was it? After some frustration you have your "Ah yes" moment.

Memories can be highly selective. People who wonder in mid-life how they will ever survive their many trials and disappointments may attest later in life that, if they had to live over again, they would not change a thing. What became of those burdens they felt unbearable?

Memories often rely on association of things or events. Try this on your friends. Read to them a list of six associated words—for example, typical pets such as dog, parakeet, rabbit, ferret, canary, and hamster. Leave out cat. Ask your friends to repeat back as many of the associated words as they can recall. Several can be expected to mention cat.

Eyewitnesses frequently have conflicting recollections. This is demonstrated especially following a traumatic event. Was the falling airplane on fire before it crashed or did striking the building cause it to burn? At the family reunion, did Uncle Elmer accidently spill wine on the linen table cloth, or was it Aunt Nell?

It is not older people alone who have unreliable memories. Young, brilliant people experience memory problems. In writing the biography of computer-entrepreneur Steve Jobs, Walter Isaacson complained that "Steve would tell me the same story three or four times, and each time it would be a little different." Sound familiar? This common trait has made life a bit easier for trial lawyers, if not biographers.

Bob Woodward is a successful author of many books dealing with political matters. He and Carl Bernstein earned fame and respect as *Washington Post* reporters for their "Deep Throat" articles on the Watergate scandal. Much later there was a well-publicized dispute about Woodward's remembrance of his claimed interview with William J. Casey, President Reagan's former Director of the CIA, at Casey's hospital deathbed. Casey's widow said her husband, dying of a brain tumor, could not communicate at that time. Circumstances are recalled quite differently by those directly involved.

Sympathy and bias affect our memories. In your teen years did your parents seem unfairly judgmental and woefully uninformed, only to unaccountably gain wisdom as they aged? Did the sibling who caused you annoyance in your childhood become transformed for those years in your later memory—especially when that person was stricken by a serious illness or passed away.

As we tread the road of life, we lighten those memories surrounded by dark shadows. We recall them in the sunlight of our journey's extended mile posts. Proceed with the memories that bring you a smile, perhaps a barely-audible chortle. Those who notice your quizzical behavior will wonder what is on your mind. Let them know. Some of our half-remembered ordinary days become "those good old days."

8

WITHERING PENSIONS AND ENCORE CAREERS

Older workers are retiring later. Uncertainty about their retirement funds, the rising costs of health care, and a desire to remain active all contribute to this trend.

Workers 55 years of age and older represent an increasing share of the labor force. Participation rates for others, particularly the youthful, have declined since the recession that began in 2008. The labor-force rate of participation is defined, by the Bureau of Labor Statistics (BLS), as "the fraction of individuals within a specific group who are working or actively pursuing work."

In 1993 only 29.4% of those 55 years of age and older were in the labor force. By 2010 their participation rate rose to 40.2 percent—the highest level over the 1975-2000 period—where it remained in 2011, according to the BLS. The rate for those 65 years of age or older rose also, from 13.7% in 1975 to 17.9% in 2011.

Lack of confidence in the adequacy of retirement funds has been a leading incentive in delaying retirement. The Employee Benefit Research Institute (EBRI), in its March

2011 survey entitled "Retirement Confidence Survey," found that 27% of workers are "not at all confident" about their retirement finances, compared to 22% of workers surveyed in the EBRI's 2010 report. The 2010 survey found "workers are more pessimistic than at any time in the two decades the survey has been conducted." Only 13% of workers in the 2010 survey felt "very confident of a comfortable retirement."

From the end of World War II through 1973, American companies generally provided attractive pension benefits, called "defined-benefit retirement programs." From 1973 forward workers increasingly have had to invest in 401-(k) "defined-contribution retirement programs," in which they assume personal responsibility for their defined-contribution investment risks.

The Australian Centre for Financial Studies ranked the viability of sampled pension funds among 16 industrialized countries. In 2009 the U.S. ranked sixth, dropping to ninth in 2011, at which time it was given a score of 58.1 for a grade of "C." A score between 65 and 79 earns a "B" grade. In 2011 no country earned an "A" grade, which begins with a score of 80. The Netherlands ranked first among the countries with 77.9 points.

A "C" grade indicates the pension system has "some desirable features, but also has major weaknesses and/or omissions that need to be addressed," according to the Centre.

An organization called ReServe is a non-profit founded in 2005 to assist workers, ages 55 or older, in securing part-time employment in non-profit and government agencies. The work pays $10 per hour. Workers age 66 years or older comprised 55% of ReServe participants in late 2011. For the five years ended 2011, ReServe reports that "1,300 individuals have held assignments in more than 350 organizations, providing more than 714,000 hours of service."

ReServe began its employment assistance in New York City, expanding later to Westchester County (NY), Newark (NJ), Miami, and the Milwaukee area. A presence is planned in Boston. The organization is funded by private and public grants plus donations from individuals.

There is another type of "reserve" that may benefit older workers seeking employment. That would be the reserve of specialized skills and talents possessed by senior citizens. Several state governments have reduced their financial support of universities and colleges, causing reductions in computer science, engineering, and nursing studies. Faced with declining state revenues, the budget authorities reason that students graduating in these majors enjoy good paying jobs and, hence, should pay more for their education.

The Center for the Study of Education Policy at the University of Illinois reports that among all 50 states, the combined financing for state higher education fell from $75.37 billion in FY 2007 to $72.48 billion in FY 2012. As some states increased their 2007-2012 financial support for higher education, others reduced financing by 10% or more. The latter states include Arizona, California, Florida, Louisiana, Nevada, New Mexico, Pennsylvania, South Carolina, and Washington.

Students who wish to pursue career studies in fields where budgets have been reduced may be denied the opportunity to matriculate if they lack financial support. The gap in qualified workers may have to be filled from the ranks of those who choose to postpone retirement.

Comedian George Burns worked until he died at the age of one-hundred. One of his most-remembered remarks is: "Retirement at 65 is ridiculous. When I was 65, I still had pimples." He loved his vocation and did not consider it work. It was enjoyment. How could he retire if he wasn't working?

9

ENHANCING OUR HEARING

If you had to choose between losing your sight or your hearing, which would it be? Helen Keller, who was both blind and deaf, observed that losing sight means you lose contact with objects, while the loss of hearing means you lose contact with people.

Herman Melville rated the value of hearing when one of his characters, in his slightly-known novel, <u>Pierre</u>, advised that "What we take to be our strongest tower of delight only stands at the cusp of the minutest event: the falling of a leaf, the hearing of a voice…" We might add, too, the serenade of a song bird, the ripple of a brook, the cooing of an infant.

We who are hearing-impaired lose the beauty of the "minutest events" when we avoid hearing aids. Eye glasses are an entirely different matter. We think of them as ubiquitous and somewhat fashionable. Hearing aids, in contrast, are resisted by some who feel they are a stigma reserved for the aged. The true stigma lies in not hearing what is being said.

A study by Johns Hopkins University concluded that six out of seven Americans, age 50 or over, who have a hearing loss, do not wear hearing aids. If the reason is vanity, and not cost, other trends ironically favor hearing-assistive ear attachments. Look around and note the number of young and middle-age who wear ear buds, headphones and Bluetooth devices.

Hearing aids worn by celebrities popularize their acceptability. When President Reagan began wearing hearing aids in 1983, the devices received a big sales boost. President Clinton's use of hearing aids, at the age of 51, spurred sales among Baby Boomers. And there are other celebrities who wear hearing aids and have contributed to their acceptability. Among them are Rosalyn Carter, Sally Fields, Arnold Palmer, and Richard "John Boy" Thomas.

According to the American Speech-Language Hearing Association (ASHA), about one-third of those 65 years old experience some age-related hearing loss, which the professionals call "presbycusis" (prez-bee-KU-sis). This condition will affect "more than 50% of those over 80 years of age" reports the Hearing Research Center at the University of Washington. More men than women experience this disability.

Presbycusis, a descriptor combining presby (elder) and cusis (hearing), indicates a loss of hearing due to damage to the hair cells of the inner ear. Unlike the hair cells on our scalp or eye-brows, these hair cells are highly developed "end-stage cells" and can't grow back.

What causes damage to these hair cells? Noise, for one thing. Noise is measured in decibels (dB). A normal conversation, for example, measures about 60 dB. Every additional 10 dB doubles the noise level. Noise exceeding 85 dB over a prolonged period is the threshold to avoid if these hair cells are to be protected. Rock concerts, sporting events, movie theatres, and some MP3 players (at full volume), at times, exceed 100 dB.

Restaurants can be annoyingly loud. Tom Sietsema, who reviews Washington, DC-area restaurants for the *Washington Post*, includes decibel readings in his reports. For example, one review reads: "71 dB, must speak with raised voice." Another reads: "86 dB, extremely loud." The noise level is a standard feature of his reviews. (Would that he add lighting levels, such as "menu impossible to read without a flashlight.")

Industry and government sources have partnered to provide means by which an audio signal is converted to a readable text. The Television Decoder Circuitry Act mandated that, beginning in 1993, all new television screens 13 inches or larger be equipped to display closed-circuit captioning. The display is "closed," that is, it is provided only if the viewer activates this option.

Closed-circuit captioning is particularly attractive in family settings at home to include the hearing-impaired in the enjoyment of shared viewing. Captioning also is used in sport bars where ambient noise makes the television audio difficult to comprehend for almost everyone.

"Next Generation 9-1-1" service operators can receive text messages from wireless subscribers who are hearing impaired. This emergency-communications accessibility began in 2009 with a successful pilot program in Black Hawk County, Iowa (population 132,000).

Smart phones, tablet computers and MP3/iPods are available with various applications ("apps") to enhance incoming sound or convert it to text. There is a market lag in seeing these apps deployed among users. The elderly typically are not smart-phone subscribers.

As Baby Boomers turn elderly, and their hearing diminishes, their acceptance of these "apps" is likely to expand broadly.

There is one caveat. The assistance of an audiologist is prudent to assure that the app selected has acceptable characteristics, both in the level of amplification and the range of frequencies it manages.

These and other devices have greatly advanced assistive hearing technologies from the time when the state-of-the art was represented by the primitive ear trumpet. That device, tubular with a funnel at one end, directed sound waves to the ear of the wearer. Ear trumpets date back to at least the second century AD. They continued to be marketed until about 1920.

There are occasions where it seems apparent the aged pretend not to hear. President George Herbert Walker Bush admitted in an interview, televised June 2012, that he used this ruse on occasion to ignore unwanted questions or statements.

10

CHIVALRY IS NOT ENTIRELY DEAD

Chivalry is not entirely dead. As a formal institution, it languished long ago. Gunpowder and the passing of feudalism eliminated the need for knights in armor. But noble instincts survive, as do archaic vestiges of titled knighthood.

Charles Kingsley (1819-1875), included this observation in his prolific writings: "Some say that the age of chivalry is past, that the spirit of romance is dead. The age of chivalry is never past, so long as there is a wrong left un-redressed on earth."

Those who practice chivalry's values constitute today's informal legions of nobility. Chivalry of these modern "knights" manages to co-exist with the knavery of rascals and rogues, despite being overwhelmed by the sheer numbers of the latter.

Chivalry and knighthood date back to the fifth and early sixth centuries A.D. Remnants of royal institutions of knighthood exist to this day. Prince William, for example, was enrolled in 2008 as the 1,000[th] Knight of the Garter since that order was established in 1349 by King Edward III. Today the Austrian House of Hasburg and the King of Spain each appoints Knights of the Order of the Golden Fleece, an institution that originated in 1430. To be a proud knight in an order curiously named either "Garter" or "Fleece," one should be armored with remarkable fortitude.

High ethical values were expected of knights in armor, such as fidelity to church and sovereign, valor, fighting fair, and protecting the weak—especially damsels. But historians have concluded that knights of old did not necessarily embody today's romanticized versions of such conduct.

If a knight spared the life of an opponent, it was not out of gallantry but to obtain a promise from the defeated to pay the victor a "ransom" sum. Their code of honor applied primarily to members of their own class, not to social inferiors. When knight fought knight, certain rules of combat applied. "Liberty, equality and fraternity" would be anathema to their sense of aristocracy. Pillaging and ravaging by them were not always restrained.

The ethics and honor of medieval knights distinguishes them in mythology from the behavior of the lesser classes. But there was no uniform conduct code of knighthood. It evolved over time and location. "The ultimate shapes that it took in practice were due to the choices made by the knights themselves," according to a paper authored by Dr. Richard Abels, of the U.S. Naval Academy.

In the United States we have the legacy of codes of chivalrous standards. They extend from the Pledge of Allegiance, the Boy Scouts Oath, the Six Pillars of Character Counts, and the cultural norms of Southern hospitality. While these codes may influence our declared values, they do not always force our instinctive conduct.

How do you account for the reactions of males aboard the sinking Titanic (1912)? They often made way to have women and children the first to secure refuge on life boats. In sharp contrast, males aboard the sinking Lusitania (1915) looked first for their own safety. Some believe the 2 hours and 40 minutes that passed before the stricken Titanic sank gave male passengers time to reflect on their sense of honor in conducting themselves altruistically.

It took only 18 minutes for the Lusitania to sink, creating a sudden panic with every man looking out for himself. The two incidents, occurring only three years apart, illustrate the co-existence of chivalry and knavery given similar catastrophes.

In 2012, one hundred years after the Titanic tragedy, Francesco Schettino, captain of the cruise liner Costa Concordia, in saving himself, allegedly abandoned passengers to the hazards of going under with the half-sunken ship. The example of Edward Smith, captain of the Titanic, who went down with his ship, reportedly was lost on Captain Schettino.

An obligation to honorable conduct is not explained simply by the amount of time available to contemplate one's reaction. A combat soldier who throws himself on a live grenade to shield other members of the squad has no time to reflect on honor and duty. In doing so, one acts on instinct alone.

What engenders instinct so extraordinary that it overpowers the primal sense of self preservation? It seems heroism resides in one's heart without conscious deliberation. It is a virtue waiting for an unanticipated opportunity to emerge.

We see heroic instinct among firefighters and police. Firefighters entered the inferno of the North Tower of the World Trade Center on September 1, 2001, after the South Tower had already collapsed. Approximately 250 of the North Tower "first responders" died trying to rescue others.

Cory Becker, mayor of Newark, NJ, instinctively ran into a burning building (2012) to save the life of a woman who most certainly would have perished without Mayor Becker's heroic instinct. Nurse Clara Barton comforted Civil War combatants, disregarding her own safety.

There is a nobility of character that is often expressed by the French phrase *Noblesse Oblige*—the obligation of nobles, and those of noble character, to be of service to others. Power resides in noble character, and with power comes obligations.

11

ON FADING AWAY

Life is a paradox. We begin to live and we begin to die at the moment of birth. Every passing day is both a renewal and a fading of life.

St. Jerome (342-420) said: "Every day we are changing, every day we are dying, and yet we fancy ourselves eternal." Montesquieu (1689-1755) was a bit more indelicate: "A man should be mourned at his birth, not at his death."

Life's fading was captured poetically by Crowfoot, a Blackfoot Indian chief known for his wisdom. He lived at least 70 years, dying in 1890, his birth year not recorded.

At that time reaching the age of 70 was a fairly long existence. Yet Crowfoot saw the duration of human life as "the flash of a firefly in the night, the breath of a buffalo in the wintertime, the little shadow which runs across the grass and loses itself in the sunset."

Live life the way you should have lived when it is time for your "little shadow" to lose itself in the sunset. When you approach the heavenly gates, you want to bring with you a commendable resume. Deathbed conversions are not recommended as a substitute for a life of virtue.

We know when a person is dead. Often we do not know if a person is dying. Pocahontas died unexpectedly at the age of 21. It is believed she died of a broken heart upon learning that her true love, John Smith, was alive and married. She had been told by her husband, John Rolfe, that Smith was deceased.

Jack Carson is another example. The popular character actor (1910-1963) died knowing he had terminal stomach cancer. He did not tell anyone "how truly grave his condition was," according to his manager. Was Carson's stoicism admirable, or did he fail an obligation to prepare his friends and family of his impending demise.

There is the romantic allure of a prompt after-life reunion when spouses die only days apart. The suggestion of unbearable grief as the cause of the survivor's passing is a compelling testimony to an inseparable bond.

Death is inevitable for all creations and creatures. As individuals we anticipate our mortality. The human race itself will end at some point and, eventually the earth and, in another five billion years or so, the sun.

Death is the law of life. Only an atheist firmly believes in the finality of death. For the religious, death is a transition to eternal life.

Many of us do not transition willingly as we journey through life. We seek comfort in continuing with what we have—our memories, our possessions, our relations, yesterday's sameness. When the infirmities of age arrive, we lack the experience of having renewed ourselves as we go through life's sequences. If we have not prepared ourselves for the final sequence, we feel helpless and bewildered.

Each successive stage presents the opportunity to transition to our new self. Continuity of habit does not preserve us. It retards our development.

With a bizarre sense of humor, the mayor of Falciano del Massico, Italy, decreed the continuity of human life in his village. He declared, March 5, 2012, that dying was against the law because the village lacked a cemetery. He explained: "The ordinance has brought happiness. Unfortunately, two citizens disobeyed the law. Citizens, while we await the construction of the new cemetery, I order you not to die so we don't have any problems." The village had seceded from a neighboring village and, by doing so, lost use of their shared cemetery.

Were you ever given a medical diagnosis that indicated your condition was potentially terminal? Elizabeth Kubler-Ross, a psychiatrist and author of <u>On Death and Dying</u> (1969), conducted extensive research on how people react to awareness of their terminal illness. She concluded there are five typical reactions: denial, anger, bargaining, despair, and acceptance. One may experience one or more of these stages, perhaps alternating between them. For example, the reaction may shift from anger to acceptance and then back again to anger. Bargaining seems an interesting reaction. "Lord, if you cure me of my cirrhosis, I swear I will not touch liquor again." When bargaining fails, anger may be the next reaction.

One response, which seems common, is for the terminally ill to reach out to others. Perhaps this is part of the "acceptance" reaction.

In the 1800s and early 1900s, a household generally held multiple generations—grandparents, their children and grandchildren. Today that is rarely the case. Now the elderly more often live independently or reside in nursing homes or assisted-living centers. Their children and grandchildren, dispersed geographically, may not witness what it means to gradually become old.

Our final sequence of life should be a time to reach out for comfort amongst our family and friends.

12

WILL SARTORIAL SPLENDOR RETURN

Does your wardrobe look like vintage clothing? If so, take pride in your garments. They show respect to your generation and to yourself. Abandonment of sartorial splendor during the past 40 years is evidence of cultural decadence. The primary offending exhibits are torn jeans, tee shirts with bawdy messages, gaudy designs, or designer logos.

But times are changing. Raising sartorial standards is inevitable. They only can be elevated, not diminished further. As long as the economy remains relatively stagnant, employment analysts believe job applicants will dress more fashionably to be competitive. Those who already have a job may subscribe to the adage: "Dress for the job you want, not the one you have."

The *Wall Street Journal* (11-17-11), citing the market-research firm NPD Group as its source, reports "men's apparel sales rose 6.5% to $53.7 billion in the year through September 2011." That is half the amount spent annually by women for their apparel—a ratio not surprising to all but the most inattentive males.

Tastes are changing. Beatle Paul McCartney, now "Sir Paul," in 2012 released several vocal recordings arranged in the syncopated ballad styles of the 1930s and 1940s, a clear departure from rock-and-roll. For example, he recorded his rendition of Thomas "Fats" Waller's classic "I'm going to sit right down and write myself a letter (and make believe it came from you)." Another rocker, Rod Stewart, led the way of recording romantic ballads in the style made famous by vocalists of the 1950s and 1960s.

Let us hope such revivals in musical tastes serve as a harbinger for the return of higher standards in wardrobe selections. The change would do wonders for our cultural landscape.

Keep those neckties, the button-down oxford shirts, your fedora hats, and the sleeveless V-neck sweaters. Don't dispose of your argyle socks. It is probably safe to throw out the suede shoes, the straw bowler, and Nehru jackets. Your tie clasps and collar pins should be examined for their gold content before dispatching them to the recycling bin. Boxer versus jockey shorts or bikini-briefs remain a matter of choice between you and your "significant other," as undergarments normally are concealed from public view.

The decline of sartorial splendor in twentieth-century America can be traced to the tieless open shirt collar. The necktie was prominent in fashions from shortly after World War I until about 1995, at which time it reached its U. S. annual sales peak of just over 100 million units. By 2001 the sales volume dropped to 60 million, declining further to 44 million in 2007. A Gallop poll found that the number of men who wore a tie to work every day dropped from 10% to 6% from 2001 to 2007. In 2008 the trade association that represented American necktie manufacturers, The Men's Dress Furnishings Association, ceased to exist.

Iran's current president, Ahmadinejad, said he goes tieless because that garment represents "western decadence." Ironically, both President Obama and Mitt Romney often chose to be tieless in their campaign appearances. The Chinese and British continue to honor the necktie in their business and social attire, keeping the tradition alive.

Officers of internet companies often appear in open-collar tieless shirts—with the possible exception of the chief financial officer, who must occasionally meet with bankers and lawyers. The latter prefer pin-striped suits, with which wearing a tie is absolutely compulsory.

Apparently, corporate officials of web-based firms feel compelled to dress casually to demonstrate their power to ignore conventional business wear. Give them credit, at least, for rejecting the ostentatious fashions of the *nouveau riche* of yesteryears.

For decades subordinates of top executives emulated the dress styles of their corporate superiors. This made it difficult to identify the well-to-do from those in lower rungs of the corporate organizational chart. Off-the-rack suits, mass-manufactured shirts, ties and shoes at affordable prices, all became difficult to distinguish from custom-made items. Corporate officialdom had to turn to monogrammed shirts, cuff links, and little-finger rings to distinguish themselves from the *hoi polloi*. These accessories are not displays of sartorial splendor but, rather, vain affectations.

The return of women's hats would be welcomed by those fond of the fashion artistry of the nineteen-fifties and sixties. Today there are segments of society that retain this attractive embellishment, including African-American ladies at church and the Red Hat Ladies at their social events.

There seems to be little public nostalgia for padded shoulders on women's dresses, real or fake furs, hats with veils, and knee-high go-go boots. Fancy handbags and ornate shoes suggest extravagance, reminiscent of Imelda Marcos' collection of accessories. Excess does not impress.

Actor Fernando Lamas (1916-1982) remarked to Johnny Carson on the *Tonight Show*, "It's better to look good than to feel good." If Mr. Lamas admired one's appearance, he would offer his signature line: "You look mahhhvelous!" It was Mr. Lamas who looked marvelous, which made him feel good. That is an aspiration for us all.

13

THE GENDER-WAR ARMISTICE

"The proper study of man is man," is an axiom largely invalidated by the social history of the second-half of the twentieth century. The axiom was the governing view long before Alexander Pope wrote that famous quote in the early 18th century.

In the past 30 years the axiom has been recast by the social and economic evolution of women. Today the proper study of mankind is women.

Consider the dynamic change in women's status—from dependency on a male-dominated society to exercising emancipation through a multitude of choices. Modern women choose whether or not to seek marriage, higher education, motherhood, employment, political positions and those trades and professions once reserved for men. Choosing and obtaining, however, often remain different odysseys.

The acquisition of the power of choice has not come easily. It took 131 years (1789-1920) before the Nineteenth Amendment to the Constitution gave women the right to vote. New Jersey, in its formative years of statehood, gave the right to vote to "all free inhabitants," but clarified its real intent in 1807 when it re-wrote its state constitution, denying the right to women.

An Equal Rights Amendment (ERA) to the Constitution was proposed in Congress in 1923 and approved by that body forty-nine years later in 1972. By 1982 the ERA failed to be ratified as an amendment by a sufficient number of states. For a time it looked like the proposed amendment would be adopted when it won approval by 35 state legislatures, but failed to reach the minimum of 38 states for ratification.

Opponents of the ERA alarmed legislatures in the unsupportive states by claiming the proposed amendment would destroy families and marriages, make women liable to a military draft and require them to be deployed in combat. The primary objective of the ERA—equal pay for equal work—seemed lost in the clash of other values.

Despite failure to ratify the amendment, women have achieved many of its goals. At the same time they have embarked into areas that opponents warned were daunting.

Women have joined men as co-breadwinners and, often, sole breadwinners. Equal pay for equal work remains, however, an unachieved key objective of the ERA movement.

To help reach this objective, more women than men are obtaining a master degree. Still, they badly lag in some fields, such as computer science and engineering.

About one-third of students seeking Master of Business Administration (MBA) degrees are women. The percentages are higher at two prestigious institutions that award MBAs. The Harvard Business School reports women will represent approximately 39% of its Year 2013 MBA graduating class. Women at the University of Pennsylvania's Wharton School made up 45% of its Year 2011 incoming class.

Still, only 12 women were chief executive officers of the "*Fortune* 500 Companies" in 2011, down from 15 in 2010. The rankings of those 12 companies ranged from 42 to 417 in the *Fortune* listing.

Opponents of ERA were right in predicting women would be placed in dangerous work. But this outcome is being decided by women who choose dangerous occupations. In New York City, 42,161 applicants took the firefighter examination in May 2012. Of these only 1,952 (5%) were women, "roughly double the number who took it in 2007, the last time the test was given" according to *The New York Times* (5-8-12). Of New York City's approximately 10,000 firefighters only 28 were female, according to the newspaper, well below the national average of 2.5% which itself is miniscule.

In 2011 women comprised 12% of police officers nationwide, the same percentage as state governors that are women, but below the 17% that comprised the U.S. Senate and House of Representatives that year.

Women are 15% of today's active-duty military. They are moving into some combat and combat-support roles in the armed service. In fighting insurgents, a modern military faces battlefields without front lines. Women can be in a combat without warning. It makes sense to train and equip them for combat so they can respond effectively.

By demonstrating competency and determination, women are becoming more comprehendible to men, although a veil of mystery continues to shield both genders from mutual understanding. Even the esteemed psychiatrist Sigmund Freud could not entirely lift the veil. In his book, <u>Psychiatry in American Life</u>, Charles Rolo quoted Freud as confessing: "The great question ... which I have not been able to answer, despite my thirty years of research into the feminist soul, is 'What does a woman want?'"

The gender cast system has evolved to a level of unfinished negotiations, creating a type of armistice to decide how we are to proceed in the coming years. While full equality remains elusive, an understanding is progressing toward such issues as shared household responsibilities, autonomous economic pursuits, and self determination free of expired social conventions.

The goals of the Equal Rights Amendment await further fulfillment by our daughters, our nieces and granddaughters. Women's rights, like all liberties, arrive in cyclical stages that do not follow a trajectory of steady progression.

14

RECONSIDERING OUR NATIONAL MOTTO

The official motto of the United States is "In God We Trust." Although it was not adopted by Congress until 1954, the motto first began to appear on our coins in 1864. It continued on some coins until 1955 when it began to appear on all new coins and notes of legal tender.

While we are likely to retain our revered national motto, the temptation to consider an alternative motto may incite the imagination of the iconoclasts among us.

Consider the merits of *Carpe Diem* as a national motto. It is short. With only nine letters it is more suitable for larger print than our current motto and, hence, offers greater readability on small coins.

Carpe Diem should not be dismissed because it is a phrase in Latin. The U.S. Marines (*Semper Fidelis*) and the U.S. Coast Guard (*Semper Paratus*) have mottos in Latin, respectively meaning: "Always Faithful," and "Always Ready."

Mottos in Latin of several states, when expressed in English, are unappealing. Maryland's motto, for example, would read "Manly Deeds, Womanly Words." Why wouldn't the reverse be true as well? California's single-word, "Eureka," is of Greek derivation meaning "I have found it!" It was adopted during the Gold Rush. The single-word motto has much more appeal than the translation, now that the rush to California has ended.

Carpe Diem can be interpreted two ways. It can mean either "enjoy the day" or "seize the day." The difference is significant. Those who believe we are motivated primarily by material gratification prefer the first of the two interpretations. To them it means live for the day. There is historic justification for this interpretation. The Roman poet, Horace, said in his original quote: *Carpe Diem, quam minimum credula postero*, or "pluck the day, trusting as little as possible in the future."

Those who prefer the alternative interpretation, "seize the day," believe we should undertake an initiative today so as to improve life tomorrow.

Thus *Carpe Diem* satisfies either school of thought—a perfect motto to hail both our indulgences and aspirations. Einstein, again to the rescue, blended a prescription of compatible views, advising us to "learn from yesterday, live for today, and hope for tomorrow."

For some religiously devout, "In God We Trust" has an unambiguous meaning. Only God knows what tomorrow brings; hence, live for today and trust in providence for your tomorrows.

Humorist Erma Bombeck recommended living for the day, or maybe the moment. She asked: "Remember all those women who passed up the dessert cart on the Titanic? Was that their last regret?"

Bobby McFerrin's popular song, "Don't Worry, Be Happy," encouraged living for the day. There is biblical justification for his verse in Matthew 6:34: "Therefore do not worry about tomorrow, for tomorrow will worry about itself. Each day has enough trouble of its own."

There can be a price to pay when living for the day. *Mardi Gras* ("Fat Tuesday") and New Year's Eve are traditional occasions to live for the day. Lent and its privations begin the day after the excesses of *Mardi Gras*, making the transition more difficult. A nagging hangover can be the regrettable consequence of over-imbibing New Year's Eve.

If events can't be controlled, the determined effort to find happiness by living today for a better tomorrow seems delusional. The sun-dial can count the hours, but it can't plan for the sun to shine.

We know from experience the sun eventually shines. It is best to plan for those tomorrows.

15

"TRUST, BUT VERIFY"

Locks are made to keep honest people honest. An experienced thief will find a way to defeat an ordinary lock.

In the absence of locks, honest people may discover temptations familiar to those who routinely suffer from moral laxity.

None of us is charged with embezzlement from a bank if we never worked for a bank. Few women yield to becoming a "lady of the evening." Many women lack marketable physical attributes and, consequently, will never be tested.

We avoid infractions of moral conduct when tempting opportunities never present themselves. Never tempted, never failing. Feeling sanctimonious about the "loathsome conduct" of others may be our leading vice.

Aside from lack of opportunity, there is another circumstance that commends us to common standards of morality. That is the culture of trust into which we were born and matured.

Dr. Robert Putnam, a Harvard professor, concludes from his studies that we do not become more trusting of others as we age. Yet today's older generations are more trusting. Dr. Putnam explains: "The key to this paradox is to ask not how old people are, but [the era] when they were young."

If today you are in your seventies or eighties, your sense of trust is likely to be greater than those who reached adulthood during the Vietnam War and Watergate eras. Trust in our public leadership and society plummeted in the 1960s and 1970s.

A survey of 2,000 adults, conducted by the Pew Research Center in 2007, supports Dr. Putnam's findings. The survey concluded that "younger adults are less trusting than are those who are middle-aged or older." One explanation the survey offers: "It could be a generational effect—today's older adults may have come of age at a time when social mores and historical events provided a more fertile seed bed for social trust."

Being more trustful, the elderly tend to be more victimized. There are several factors that make them more vulnerable. Among them are the higher probability they have significant net worth, including home ownership, savings, social security and, frequently, pensions. Once victimized, they often are reluctant to report the incident to authorities, especially if another family member is the perpetrator. If they do report financial exploitation, the perpetrator may hope for exoneration based on the common perception that older people have poor memories, dismissing the credibility of the complainant.

A study of 5,777 elderly, conducted for the National Institute of Justice in 2009 by Don Ron Acierno, a psychologist at the Medical University of South Carolina, found that 11.5% of Americans, age 60 or older, had been recent victims of financial exploitation.

ConsumerReports.org reported (11/1/2011) that 20% of seniors age 65 or older "have been the victim of financial fraud," according to a study by Infogroup/ORC. The escalated percentages cited in these two studies imply that as current elders become older, the more vulnerable they become to financial abuse.

This finding is supported by a study, sponsored by MetLife Mature Market Institute, entitled "Broken Trust: Elders, Family, and Finances" (March 2009). Their research found increasing vulnerability as today's elderly age pass their sixties. Those in their nineties are said to experience fewer incidents, however, because they may have fewer resources to plunder.

There is reason to expect future generations of elderly will be less trusting, and thus less vulnerable to financial plunder. President Reagan was correct when he advised: "Trust, but verify."

The MetLife study found the four leading perpetrators of financial abuse of the elderly are trusted professionals (18.0%), family (16.9%), non-agency care-givers (10.9%), and agency care-givers (9.3%). Ten other classifications of perpetrators accounted for the remaining 44.9 percent.

One cannot judge a person's character by appearance. Mark Twain wrote in his short story, A Mysterious Visit (1875): "Barring that natural expression of villainy, which we all have, the man looked honest enough."

16

MIND YOUR MANNERS

Our spouse, significant other, grandmother, and mother have tried to keep us mindful of our manners. Grade-school teachers often graded our "deportment" or "conduct" on report cards. But whose standards should we follow? They can evolve within a single generation.

Through the centuries, arbiters of manners attempt to guide our conduct. In the 13th Century, Daniel of Beccles wrote a guide entitled <u>Book of the Civilized Man</u>. Today it would be read mostly for amusement. His advice included these maxims: If you wish to belch, remember to look up to the ceiling; don't mount your horse in the hall; and, when eating, don't use your fingers to clean bowls. At least the last one remains valid today.

George Washington, in 1748 at the age of 16, copied the 110 rules published in the <u>Rules of Civility and Decent Behavior in Company and Conversation</u>. The origin of these rules dates to 1595 when they were compiled by French Jesuits. That is an outstanding tenure of 153 years for maintaining a single code of conduct.

Included are some rules which apply to this day. Rule #1 advises that "Every action, done in company, ought to be with some sign of respect to those that are present." Rule #5 states "If you cough, sneeze or yawn, do it not loudly but privately." One other standard with lasting validity is Rule #13, "Kill no vermin as fleas, lice, ticks, etc. in the sight of others."

Rules of proper manners evolve as circumstances change. That explains why Emily Post's first edition of Etiquette, published in 1922, is now in its eighteenth revision, a 732-page treatise issued in 2011. Ms. Post died in 1960. Updating her classic continues through her progeny, a great-granddaughter-in-law, two great-great-granddaughters, and a great-great grandson, all of whom collaborate, at times, as revision co-authors.

Emily Post, herself divorced, had this admonition in the 1922 edition: "A man of honor never seeks publicly to divorce his wife, no matter what he believes her conduct to have been; but for the protection of his name, and that of his children, he allows her to get her freedom on other than criminal grounds." The eighteenth edition has no similar guideline, apparently permitting husbands to initiate a divorce based on the conduct of the wife.

Judith Martin, who began the widely-syndicated "Miss Manners" newspaper column in 1978, is another judge of conduct. Her influence might be attributed to her gentle sense of humor.

For example, in <u>Miss Manners' Guide to Excruciatingly Correct Behavior</u> (2005), she cautions against copying the manners of a host or hostess. She wrote: "Grover Cleveland carefully added sugar and cream to his coffee, stirred it and poured some into his saucer. Observing this, all his guests felt obliged to do the same. There they all were, pouring their coffee into their saucers, when the president leaned down and put his saucer on the floor for his dog."

Are manners getting worse? In her first edition, Ms. Post equivocated on this question. "It is commonplace that older people invariably feel that the younger generation is speeding swiftly on the road to perdition." But, she concedes later, "It is difficult to maintain that youth today is so very different from what it has been in other periods of the country's history."

In that same edition, Ms. Post was concerned about such matters as the placement of ashtrays at the dinner table, a gentleman rising when a lady enters a room, and "a gentleman taking off his hat and holding it in his hand when a lady enters the elevator in which he is a passenger."

Miss Manner is convinced our manners have reached "dangerous levels." The cultural revolution of the 1960s, a time when the mood became "do-your-own-thing," seems to have been the point when public decorum began its precipitous decline.

A survey conducted in 2002, funded by the Pew Charitable Trust, may remain an accurate reflection of current opinion regarding public manners. The survey of 2,013 adults, entitled "Aggravating Circumstances: A Status Report on Rudeness in America," found that 79% of respondent "say lack of respect and courtesy should be regarded as a serious national problem. Six in ten believe the problem is getting worse."

Another survey, conducted by Public Agenda in 2002, identified leading behavioral annoyances. The list seems as current today as it was over a decade ago, citing aggressive driving, out-of-control parents at youth sport events, loud and annoying cell phone conversations, crude or nasty e-mails, foul-language, and littering as the more noxious offenses.

What is your practice in observing manners? Do you generally favor greeting a friend by a kiss on the cheek, embracing, extending a one-armed "bro-hug," a high-five, a handshake, or a fist-bump? When noting a special occasion, do you e-mail a graphic found on the internet or do you mail a printed greeting card via the U.S. Postal Service?

When dining in public as a couple, does the male pull out the preferred chair for the female? Does the male open and shut the car door for his female passenger? When dining in a group, do you wait until everyone is served before eating? Does the male walk on the curb-side of a sidewalk to shield the female from water sprays caused by passing traffic? Do you speak quietly in a library?

Responses to the foregoing questions may reflect your generation and its customs. What is acceptable to one generation may be offensive to another—for example: Is he a classic gentleman or a male chauvinist when showing consideration to women?

Sensing the correct approach during many uncertain circumstances may be one path to succeeding socially, as attempted by the teen-aged George Washington in his effort to achieve "civility and decent behavior in company and conversation."

17
SWEARING

Without uttering a single profanity, we nevertheless swear our way through life. Pledges, oaths, covenants, vows, and commitments are obligations by which we swear our personal affirmation.

Such sworn obligations start early in life—perhaps as the Boy Scout Oath or the Girl Scout Promise—and extend into our senior years. Renewal of marriage vows upon a couple's Golden Anniversary is one example of the latter.

There is no escaping our swearing. With the exception of a few religious minorities and anarchists, most of us have recited the Pledge of Allegiance. Some states require making the Pledge to begin the school day. City-council meetings and lodge meetings often begin with the Pledge. When we pledge allegiance, we swear our allegiance.

Hebrew children undergo a formal commitment to obey the commandments. At the age of 13 for boys and 12 for girls, the children are deemed to have reached the age of reason, responsible for their personal conduct. A formalized commitment is a sworn pledge.

The Boy Scout Oath is a promise, on one's honor, to do one's best, to do one's duty to God and country, to obey the Scout Law, to help other people at all times, to keep oneself physically strong, mentally awake and morally straight. That burden of sworn responsibilities would test the strength of a saint.

The Girl Scout Oath seems much more lenient. It simply requires that the scout, on her honor, "will try to serve God and my country, to help people at all times, and to live by the Girl Scout Law."

As we proceed through life there are numerous oaths we encounter. In the matrimonial ceremony the traditional pledge is "to love, cherish, honor, and keep or respect in sickness and in health as long as both shall live." Today a couple may chose to recite an oath they have composed, possibly amending or deleting some of these time-honored words.

If you testify in a trial, you may be asked to swear to "tell the truth, the whole truth, and nothing but the truth, so help you God." When enlisting or re-enlisting in the army, you are required to take an oath in which you swear to support and defend the Constitution of the United States against all enemies, obey the orders of the President and of the officers appointed over you. Amending or deleting any of these obligations is not an option.

If elected to public office, one is "sworn-in." To display allegiance to our country, many male politicians at the federal level wear a flag pin on their suit lapel. It signifies nothing. Scoundrels have been known to wrap themselves in the flag.

Millions of Americans live in communities governed by homeowner or condominium associations. Part of their home-purchase process is acceptance of the community's "Covenants, Conditions, and Restrictions," commonly called the CCR Document. This document obligates the homeowner to comply with the associations rules and architectural guidelines. If charged with a CCR violation, the homeowner cannot plead a defense stating the content of the document had not been read.

Our pledges, oaths, and commitments are, too often, regarded as unavoidable formalities to the real business at hand: getting a meeting underway, buying a home, giving testimony, marrying, and more. We regard them as inconveniences, not an expression of convictions.

Former Governor Jesse Ventura, in 2002, vetoed a bill requiring the Pledge of Allegiance to be recited in Minnesota public schools at least once a week. Responding with more candor than political discretion, the governor explained: "I believe patriotism comes from the heart. Patriotism is voluntary. There is much more to being a patriot than reciting the Pledge or raising the flag. Patriots serve. Patriots vote. Patriots attend meetings in their community. No law will make a citizen a patriot."

The most profoundly-moving oath in the history of our nation appears in the Declaration of Independence. The signers courageously stated: "And for the support of this Declaration, with a firm reliance on the protection of Divine Providence, we mutually pledge to each other our lives, our fortunes, and our sacred honor." Rallying the public to separate from the mother country was treasonous, subjecting each of them to the gallows if they failed.

While our oaths and pledges typically are empty gestures, the informal resolutions we make and keep are more meaningful. They govern how we conduct our everyday life.

We can resolve not to abuse parking reserved for the handicapped, not to allow our dog to relieve itself on the property of others, not to embellish expenses when computing our taxes, not to go to the head of a waiting line when exiting our vehicle at a highway off-ramp, and countless other obligations to civility.

18

MIRACLES AND WONDERS

Skeptics deny or doubt the possibility of miracles. Miracles are unexplained phenomena that seem to violate natural laws.

We readily acknowledge that extraordinary or inexplicable wonders do exist, some of which may be designated as miracles by the spiritually-minded. The northern light, lightning and thunder—all natural wonders—may have been regarded by primitive people as the presence of a divinity or an evil spirit. Despite scientific explanations, there remains, for many of us, a blurred line between miracles and enigmatic wonders.

Man-made physical wonders, such as the Colossus of Rhodes, a 110' tall statute, or the 425' tall Lighthouse of Alexandria, are curiosities built about 300 BC that defy understanding. How could they be built without cranes and graduate M.I.T. engineers? If even man-made wonders cannot be explained, can we confidently rule out the possibility of miracles occurring in other phenomena?

Life is a wonder, if not a miracle, all of life—every facet of it. The seasons are possible and predictable because our planet revolves around the sun at a prescribed orbit. Days and nights are due to the rotation around the sun of the earth on its axis. These are natural wonders which we accept without much thought given to the extraordinary, odds-defying requisite conditions that make earth inhabitable.

Consider gravity, which is calibrated for us at the precise intensity to allow us to walk confidently, instead of floating above or bouncing on the planet's surface. Or fire, which blooms spontaneously once flammable material is touched by an igniting agent. These wonders are not readily understandable, but they rarely are attributed as miracles.

The genes of animals compel them to exhibit instinctive behavior at birth, which is unexplainable. Our complex minds marvel at how a creature as tiny as a fruit fly can outwit us when they are about to be swatted, causing them to escape doom in a split-second maneuver.

And how is it that 7 billion people living on earth today each have an individually identifiable face, voice, and finger prints? Michelle de Montaigne, the writer credited as the first essayist, wrote "If our faces were not similar, we could not distinguish man from beast; if they were not dissimilar, we could not distinguish man from man (his Book 3, "Of Experience").

The universe is an awesome creation, if only that part which we can see. An estimated 4% of its material is visible to us. We don't understand the remaining unseen 96%, which we call "dark matter" and "dark energy."

Scientists announced, July 2012, discovery of what they believe is the presence of the elusive "Higgs Boson," the function of which is believed to give mass to elementary particles. We search for the answer as to how the particles that comprise our bodies, and everything about us, are able to bind together. Higgs may explain the process with his theory. Until we comprehend the boson, we can't conclude that we have identified a miracle or an understandable natural wonder.

Such weighty matters are left to brilliant scientific minds, not to us mere mortals. Ordinary humans have difficulty understanding the possibility of both ancient and modern man-made creations.

How is it possible, for example, that a Boeing 747 airliner, with an empty weight of 400,000 pounds and a maximum take-off weight of 800,000 pounds, can leave the ground and fly, as Frank Sinatra crooned, "up there where the air is rarified."

If Thomas Edison, who clearly had a brilliantly inquisitive mind, was foretold of a flying 747, he would have insisted that the authorities confine his informant to an asylum.

Mother Nature is custodian of an incalculable number of wonders, many of which we may never understand. The study of phenomena that defy our understanding leads to creativity in developing products and processes.

Miracles and wonders, such as the sun's continuing inferno and mankind's splitting of the atom, are entwined, leaving us the potential beneficiaries as we explore their inter-linked explanations. We should not relegate everything we regard as a miracle to an off-limits *sanctum sanctorum*, divinely authored but insulated from our investigation. The quest for unlocking all of life's unexplained wonders is at the center of mankind's temporal mission.

19

OUR DIVISIBLE NATION

A growing Hispanic population is forecast to become our country's largest single ethnicity by 2050, based on current trends. How likely is it that the Canadian model of two autonomous linguistic groups, separated culturally and geographically, will be officially adopted in the United States?

Several terms are used to describe the dynamics of our multicultural nation. Decades ago we preferred to think assimilation of culture made us *E Pluribus Unum*. Then immigration and birth-rate patterns produced other characterizations, generally described as "pluralistic." Some argue the blend of the symbolic melting pot has been replaced by the salad bowl and its ingredient variations.

Hispanics were 6.6% of the nation's population in 1980. The Census Bureau forecast that this ethnicity will triple, from 50 million in 2011 to 133 million by 2050, up from 16% to 30% of our projected population.

Racially, the United States has changed significantly, if not radically, during the period 1980-2011. In 1980 whites comprised 86% of the population, blacks 12% and "all others" (primarily Asian, Native Americans, and bi-racial) were 2 percent. By 2011 these shares were, respectively, 78%, 13%, and 9 percent.

Because of our cultural heritage, peopled even during colonial days by a broad-mix of ethnicities, we continue to think of the majority of our nation's population as Euro-centric. That perception will change as variations in the salad-bowl demographics become increasingly apparent. Minorities account for 50.4% of the nation's population under the age of 1, as of July 2011, according to the Census Bureau. (The Pew Research Center defines "minorities" as anyone other than a single-race non-Hispanic white.)

Given its growing cultural divisions, our nation may be facing a divided house that Lincoln struggled to prevent some 7 score years ago. Many nations are divided by cultures, not always amicably. The European Union officially recognizes 23 languages among its members. Canada provides an example of a strained co-existence with only 2 major ethnicities.

At its federal level, Canada has two official languages: English and French. Acts of Parliament, for example, must be published in both languages even though 8 of its 10 provinces have populations in which more than 90% speak English as their only language or primary language. The Province of Quebec is monolingual by law, with French its official language. Bilingualism has not been widely established in Canada.

From the 1960s through 1995, Quebec was engaged in a sovereignty movement that sought a negotiated exit from federalism, paving the way for Quebec to become an independent country. Most Quebecers recognize, however, that if separation was achieved this newly independent country would continue to depend on the use of the Canadian currency and military. Both conditions were tangled in complications.

Two referenda in Quebec, one in 1980 and the other in 1995, rejected separation. The referendum of 1995 had a slim majority of 50.6% opposing separation. Thereafter the sovereignty movement exhausted its political energy. The mood because one of increased autonomy, avoiding complete independence.

As the future demographics of the United States seem apparent, the need to understand each other's language is underscored. Despite our chorus of mixed languages, we Americans are the least bilingual of the major countries.

Failing to promote bilingualism raises the probability that, like Canada, the United States will evolve into two geographically identifiable ethnic zones, with Hispanics dominant from California through the southwest and eastward to include Florida.

English-speaking Americans will continue to dominate, into the mid-21st century, the states bordering Canada, from Washington to Maine, plus the Midwest, southern and mid-Atlantic regions. These two zones, each essentially monolingual by mid-century, eventually will lapse into a confederation of two autonomous, if not independent, nations.

Our past expectation that immigrants would assimilate into homogeneous Americans was a goal expressed by President Theodore Roosevelt, when he remarked: "We have room for but one language here, and that is the English language, for we intend to see that the crucible turns our people out as Americans, of American nationality, not as dwellers in a polyglot boarding house; and we have room for but one loyalty, and that is loyalty to the American people."

Today Teddy might forego an insistence on one language and settle for one allegiance to a polyglot country under one flag.

20

ACHIEVING THE AMERICAN DREAM

Healthy senior citizens who arrived into their retirement years with a paid-off house mortgage, their appliances in good condition, free of meaningful credit debt, and with no children, grandchildren or parents to support, have achieved an American Dream many would envy.

John Truslow Adams, who created the term "American Dream" in his best-selling book, <u>Epic of America</u> (1931), saw the Dream as a life "better and richer and fuller for everyone, with opportunity for each according to ability or achievement …." In the early stage of the Great Depression, at which time his book was released, it was hard to perceive the Dream simply as a matter of attaining more possessions.

Long before Adams book, Americans had an American Dream. The Bill of Rights (1793) granted us three fundamental freedoms: speech, press, and religion. The Declaration of Independence claimed for "all men … certain unalienable rights, that among these are life, liberty, and the pursuit of happiness." Financial security is not a right specified in either of these documents.

A survey conducted for the Pew Center on the "Economic Mobility Project" (5-19-11) found that the highest-ranking aspiration sought by respondents was "being free to accomplish anything." Becoming rich ranked eleventh among the surveyed priorities.

If becoming excessively wealthy is the crux of the American Dream, only the famed one-percent of our population has achieved it. They are the 3.1 million millionaires, according to data reported by the *Wall Street Journal* (6-22-11). That newspaper's definition of "millionaire" excluded the value of one's "primary home, collectibles, consumables and consumer durables." The super successful are the American billionaires, of whom there were 412, or one for every 750,000 Americans as of March 2011, according to Wikipedia.

What has become of the American Dream for ordinary Americans? We have learned over the years that no economic theory or political administration has shown how to banish the business cycle. The best we can hope to accomplish is to moderate the severity of its swings.

Consider the past century. There was an economic depression from 1919 to 1921. Especially depressed was the agricultural sector, as grain exports fell sharply following the end of World War I.

Since the Great Depression of the 1930s we have had recessions in 1958-1961, others in 1973 and 1980, and the recession that began in 2008, which some call the Great Recession.

Our American forebears were encouraged to believe in their economic dreams by the Homestead Acts (1862, 1909 and 1916), which offered abundant resources waiting to be exploited. The nation enjoyed periods of economic growth insulated from international competition, as it witnessed emergence of the electric grid, automobiles, paved roads and home appliances.

Uninterrupted economic growth seemed possible following World War II, with the formation of many new households, a baby boom, and a pent-up demand that had been restrained by war-time shortages as savings accumulated and credit became widely available.

Various solutions have been suggested to resurrect America's prosperity. Bringing back manufacturing, returning agriculture to family farming, stimulating research and development, and rebuilding our infrastructure are among such proposals. Each is considered briefly in paragraphs that follow.

The Bureau of Labor Statistics reports that in 1960 one-third of U.S. employment was in manufacturing. Today it is 9 percent. While we succeed in bringing back some automobile production, the manufacture of lower-priced consumer items, such as electronics and appliances, is unlikely to return soon.

The future for making and assembling products is trending towards robotics, a technology led by our military needs and adopted by growing numbers of consumer-product manufacturers here and abroad.

Returning agriculture to family farming has benefits other than economic. The "Market Gardens"—small-scale farming with products sold directly to consumers and restaurants—provide healthful vegetables and fruits produced locally. Less than 2% of employed Americans today depend on farming for their primary income. Doubling that percentage, while impressive, would not represent a significant increase in employment numbers.

Product research and development could generously promote new and expanded businesses if the innovations are not captured by foreign suppliers. We have seen, too, that increases in employee productivity restrain gains in job growth otherwise sparked by new products.

Repairing and rebuilding our infrastructure, especially bridges, roads, and water- and sewage-pipelines, has strong public support. The enormity of the costs, as government faces revenue constraints, continues their delay.

The business cycle will accelerate its growth rate once consumer credit rises in response to increased economic confidence. Swollen funds currently cached by businesses will reappear as capital investments. The cycle will surge, peak, and then begin another descent. We have seen this many times.

A Pew Center survey (8-22-12) reported that "about 63% of the general public agree that most people who want to get ahead can make it if they're willing to work hard, [but this is] down from 74% of the public who believed so in 1999." Looking back, the older generations may conclude they were born in the best of times to experience their own American Dream.

21

FIRST LADIES AS ASSOCIATE PRESIDENTS

When we elect our country's president, we also "elect" a First Lady or First Gentleman who may have an undeclared agenda to promote. In effect, we could elect an "Associate President."

Novelist and essayist Nora Ephron recognized this possibility in a comment she made in 1983: "Women are being considered as candidates for vice president of the United States because it is the worst job in America. It's amazing that men will take it. A job with real power is First Lady. I'd be willing to run for that."

The political influence of a president's wife on her husband became evident in the administration of our second president. Mrs. John (Abigail) Adams was the First Lady who "thought herself less Lady and more co-president" according to Carl Sferrazza Anthony's book, <u>First Ladies</u>.

Anthony states that the earliest the term "First Lady" appeared in the press was October 1860, ironically during the presidential term of bachelor James Buchanan, referring to his niece, Harriet Lane. Lane at times served as hostess of the Executive Mansion. "First Lady" appeared next in a press article of August 1861, referring to Mary Lincoln.

Influential First Ladies occupied the Executive Mansion during several administrations of the 19th century. In the 20th century the second wife of President Wilson, Edith, was the first to exercise "Associate President" political influence on her husband, beginning as early as his inauguration in 1917. She reportedly persuaded the president to assign his confidant, Colonel House, as Ambassador to England so she could exercise her direct influence without the Colonel's interference. Mrs. Wilson virtually became acting president following Mr. Wilson's stroke.

Sixty-six years later Nancy Reagan asserted similar influence by effectively moving to have President Reagan's chief of staff, Donald Regan, replaced with a former senator, Howard Baker.

Michelle Obama may not have caused Chief of Staff Rahm Emanuel to resign to run for mayor of Chicago, but probably was relieved when he did so. Jodi Kantor reported in her book, The Obamas (2012), that First Lady Michelle and Emanuel had a tense relationship.

The 20th century First Lady recognized most prominently by the public as a de-facto chief assistant to the president, if not Associate President, is Eleanor Roosevelt. Because of Franklin Roosevelt's paraplegic handicap following a bout with polio, Mrs. Roosevelt travelled extensively, meeting with all levels of people, becoming her husband's "eyes and ears." Many regarded her as casting a model to which future First Ladies should aspire. Not all did.

Mamie Eisenhower appeared to be inactive politically. President Eisenhower remarked that First Lady Mamie was "my invaluable, my indispensable, but publicly inarticulate lifelong partner." When the president had a heart attack in his first term of office, Mamie recommended he not seek reelection. "Ike" rejected that advice.

Hillary Clinton and Rosalynn Carter appear to be the closest successors to Eleanor Roosevelt's model of First Lady. Hillary Clinton's activism actually exceeded the bounds established by Mrs. Roosevelt. Shortly following her husband's election, Mrs. Clinton launched a health-care task force to advocate reform legislation. The group she led consisted of almost 600 participants, chosen from governmental and private sources.

Her critics claimed that First Lady Hillary was not a government employee and, hence, should not have authority over the task force. No one should have been surprised by her ambition, considering that Bill Clinton advised in his campaign that his teamwork with his wife constituted a "two-for-one" offer.

Rosalynn Carter was also an activist as First Lady, travelling to collect information and serving as her husband's sounding board and partner. Jimmy Carter acknowledged that "there is seldom a decision that I make I don't discuss with her, tell her my opinion and seek her advice." The president invited her to attend cabinet meetings.

Mrs. Carter viewed mental health as her primary activity. Unlike Mrs. Clinton, Mrs. Carter became only the *honorary* chair of the Commission on Mental Health, whose appointees were named by President Carter.

Several First Ladies demurred from being public figures in setting government policy. Yet they may have been significant advisors to their husbands. That style of partnership was evident during the terms of presidents Harding, Hoover, Truman, Johnson, Nixon, George H.W. Bush and George W. Bush.

Two first ladies placed parenting their young children as their top priority. Jackie Kennedy and Michelle Obama held this view. Both, however, indulged subordinate interests. Mrs. Kennedy was committed to restoring historic furnishings to the White House. Mrs. Obama has promoted a campaign to find solutions for childhood obesity and to champion the needs of military families. Interview by *Parade* (9-2-12), Mrs. Obama said if her husband is reelected, a new project for her will be women's health issues.

One might assume that First Ladies, regardless of political affiliation, would be especially supportive of women's rights. Edith Wilson thought the suffragettes, those who advocated for the rights of women to vote, were "disgusting." Women won the right to vote in the 1920 presidential election when Wilson's successor, Warren Harding, became president. Harding's wife and, later, Mrs. Herbert Hoover, favored women's political and employment rights. Eleanor Roosevelt advocated appointment of women to high government positions, but felt "women have not reached enough political maturity to become president." She added "the time will come."

Mrs. Eisenhower thought women should not be appointed to key positions, asserting to her daughter-in-law, Barbara

Eisenhower, that "women who had jobs like that were very unfeminine." Mrs. Reagan was critical of the proposed Equal Rights Amendment, influencing her husband to oppose it. Mrs. Ford caused much controversy when she publicly supported the amendment, causing her to remark that she was "the only First Lady to ever have a march organized against her."

Because of their potential influence on important decisions, should the spouse of a presidential contender be required to disclose and discuss their planned projects? Retreating into semi-anonymity, the wife or husband of a nominee could lead to policy surprises once she becomes a First Lady or he a First Gentleman.

22

PROPOSED: A COUNCIL OF SAGES

Socrates spoke of the "Seven Sages," men of keen perception who were citizens of independent city states in sixth-century (BC) Greece. They never met one another and, consequently, could not have served together as a council of advisors. In this essay they serve as an inspiration for a proposed council of private citizens to advise our top elected executives.

A sage is one who is respected for experience, judgment, and wisdom. Our nation's presidents and governors would benefit the public if they each formed their own unofficial council of sagacious advisors.

The seven Greek sages generally believed humility is the basis of wisdom. A word or title other than "sage" would have to be coined should our elected executives designate unofficial councils of advisors. A truly humble person may not abide participating as a member of a Council of Sages. The word "sage" sounds pretentious, perhaps boastful.

Executive cabinets are composed of bureaucratic managers. They are heads of key departments, ostensibly appointed with other cabinet heads to develop harmonious and effective policies.

It is more likely that cabinet heads follow policy directives made by their federal or state chief executive. In turn, the chief executive follows polling data, the dictates of political alliances, lobbyists, and the recommendations of his or her spouse. This does not necessarily lead to sagacious administration.

The spouses of chief executives are consistent and candid. Opinion polls and political alliances are fickle. Outside of these sources, several modern presidents have relied heavily on a single trusted associate or friend as a sounding board, sympathetic ear, or idea generator. Nixon had "Bebe" Rebozo, Truman had General Harry Vaughn, Kennedy had Ted Sorenson, and Lyndon Johnson had Jack Valenti. Few are remembered today.

Andrew Jackson had a team of unofficial advisors, dubbed "the kitchen cabinet," on whom he depended, especially after dismissing 5 of his 8 cabinet members in the middle of his first term. Franklin D. Roosevelt needed a team of creative types in his first term. He enlisted 10 unofficial advisors as his personal "Brain Trust." In FDR's second term he reduced the number to 3 as his own pragmatic evaluations and sense of direction ripened.

In his first inaugural address, Thomas Jefferson spoke of "the wisdom of our sages and the blood of our heroes" in attaining justice, freedom, and principles applicable "to all men, of whatever state or persuasion, religious or political ..." Has the nation lacked sages in the generations that followed Jefferson's presidency? Or has history not given them the level of recognition given to our founding sages and heroes?

Who would be your nominees among 20th-century Americans who you believe to be a sage deserving of historic recognition?

Two nominees might be Dr. Walter Heller (1915-1987) and Paul Volcker (1927-   ). Heller was Chairman of the Council of Economic Advisors from 1961-1964. He promoted tax cuts, under President Kennedy, to stimulate the economy. He resigned when President Johnson, Kennedy's successor, wanted to borrow funds rather than raise taxes to pay for the war in Viet Nam.

Paul Volcker has thus far advised five presidents. He raised interest rates substantially while Chairman of the Federal

Reserve from 1979-1987, taming the inflation that occurred during the Carter and Reagan presidencies. In doing so he withstood strong opposition from affected sectors of the economy.

Distinguished for their roles in civil rights and social justice are Roy Wilkins (1901-1981), head of the NAACP, and Arnold Aronson (1911-1998). Roy Wilkins has been called "the Senior Statesman of the U.S. Civil Rights Movement." Wilkins and Aronson, together with A. Philip Randolph, founded the Leadership Conference on Civil Rights, which coordinated efforts to pass the Civil Rights Act of 1957, the Civil Rights Acts of 1964, the Voting Rights Act of 1965, and the Fair Housing Act of 1968.

Two other nominees to consider are Donald M. Nelson and Margaret Chase Smith.

The United States defeated its enemies in World War II by rapidly producing a huge arsenal of military equipment and supplies. Much of the credit for this success must be given to Donald M. Nelson (1888-1959), who was head of the War Production Board (WPB) from 1942 to 1944. During the years 1942-1945 the WPB managed production of $185 billion worth of military equipment and supplies.

Margaret Chase Smith (1897-1995), a Republican, was the first woman to serve in both houses of congress, first as a representative and then as a senator. She is remembered for her "Declaration of Conscience" speech delivered June 1, 1950, in which she refuted the inflammatory tactics launched by fellow Republican, Senator Joe McCarthy (whom she did not identify by name).

Six other senators of her party signed onto the Declaration, which eventually became a political consensus in both major parties. Senator Smith rejected the practice of placing "political exploitation above national interest."

Nominees to consider for selection as members of an unofficial council of sagacious advisers should be named in their mid-life, say up to the age of sixty. This essay does not propose a council of elders, which sometime are established in churches or in African or Native-American tribes.

Sparta (Greece) took a different view. That city state required members of its Council of Elders to be over 60 years of age. This stipulation alone seems sufficient to whittle down Sparta's list of eligible candidates to a manageable number, given the life-span in Greece at that time.

23

BATHING: NOW AND THEN

If you are physically able to do so, spend more time bathing in the bathtub or shower stall. As adults we spend about 7 hours per day sleeping (and losing consciousness), 2 hours eating (not always beneficial) and, typically, only 20 minutes of restful, hygienically-gainful, bathing or showering. That leaves 14 hours and 40 minutes for everything else. Some of that time could be allocated to more bathing or showering.

Time spent bathing or showering is the best per-minute value of the day. It gives us guiltless idleness, a time to be contemplative, free of the phone and free of idle conversations while relaxing in tranquil solitude.

Americans bathe more frequently than do residents of most other countries. That may not have been true a century ago. In 1921 only 1% of homes in this country had indoor plumbing. If one wanted to bathe, the normal practice was to do so in a portable tub which required bringing to it stove-heated water. Several family members might use the same water for the one-night-a-week bath.

Bathing weekly represents real progress compared to practices in the Middle Age. Some Christian theologians, such as St. Francis of Assisi (1181-1226), believed that cleanliness was not next to godliness. They preached that cleansing the soul was important, not the body.

Catholic philosopher St. Thomas Aquinas (1225-1274), however, strongly recommended bathing, believing it eliminated body odors which "can provoke disgust." He must have had an unusually sensitive sense of smell. When scarcely anyone bathes, pervasive body odors are tolerated as a natural phenomenon. One gets used to them.

Modern bathing practices in America began in the late 1800s. The Kohler Company in 1883 introduced its enameled claw-foot tub as a "horse trough/hog scalder, [which] when furnished with four legs will serve as a bathtub." Montgomery Ward's catalog of 1895 offered a bathtub "made of heavy cast iron, white enameled inside and painted outside." A 6-foot tub sold for $32.25. In 1900 Sears, Roebuck's catalog listed a portable tin tub for bathing, priced at $4.20. When not used for bathing, the Sears, Roebuck or the Montgomery Ward products also could be used as a trough for horses or to "scald," the latter being the removal of hair from pig skin.

There were no plumbers, commonly recognized as such, until the 1890s. Once this trade began servicing households, public health—thanks to sanitation measures brought by indoor flushing and running water—promoted disease-eradication advances as dramatically as did medical science. Toting untreated water from a well, a hydrant or a stream had been the common source of supply for most households. This undoubtedly caused fatigue, strained backs, and raised arguments as whose turn it was to tote.

Presidents John Adams (1797-1801) and Andrew Jackson (1829-1837) occasionally would go to the nearby Potomac River to bathe. Presumably, other bathers came to the river. In 1851 the first bathtub was installed in the White House, during the administration of Franklin Pierce. During Lincoln's term (1861-1865), water was piped from the Potomac to the White House.

The executive mansion currently has 35 bathrooms within its 132 rooms. We should give thanks of being assured of a sanitary chief executive in Washington, regardless who is president.

The number of bathrooms in American homes increased impressively in the past four decades. Homes with 2 or more bathrooms grew from 16% of all homes in 1970 to 87%

in 2009, according to "The American Housing Survey," conducted for the Department of Housing and Urban Development.

People may have discovered that more bathrooms within a home are not always to one's advantage. There may be a benefit of having only one bathroom—it discourages guests staying overnight and adult children living with their parents.

Bathtubs today are available with several luxurious options, attractive to people that believe the simple pleasure of bathing is not sufficient to enjoy the full potential of the experience. Options include hydro-therapy (jets of water to stimulate a massage), foot jets, chroma-therapy (underwater lighting), and aroma-therapy (injecting into the water a selected fragrance). Ordinary items, such as a tray to use as a book-or-beverage rest, and safety bars, have practical appeal that outlast frivolous indulgences.

For the elderly, a compelling option is a walk-in tub. Priced from about $3,000 to $10,000, this is more of an investment than a nonchalant extravagance. They come in various heights and features, including a whirl-pool. The investment could provide cost-recoverable value to a home as interest in these tubs is not limited to the elderly.

Water is both a spiritual and a physical experience. Baptism, holy water, and washing of hands before breaking bread on the Sabbath are spiritual values anointed through the medium of water. Relaxing in a bathtub may stir a subconscious sensation of the protective womb. Standing in a shower could invoke strains of the hymnal intonation: "wash your sins away in the tide."

The sensuous and spiritual grandeur of the bath may not be widely experienced by future generations. Inexpensive and plentiful supply of water is a fading phenomenon as century-old distribution pipes leak or burst and droughts recur more frequently.

Our grandchildren may tell their grandchildren about the good-old-days when baths were enjoyed daily. If water shortages prevail, an era of the malodorous aromas of the "Great Unwashed" could return.

Benefits of the bathtub were expressed by essayist Edmund Wilson in his A Piece of My Mind (1956): "I have had a good many more uplifting thoughts, creative and expansive visions—while soaking in comfortable baths or drying myself after bracing showers—in well equipped American bathrooms than I have ever had in any cathedral."

Mr. Wilson apparently, like most of us, spent much more time in bathrooms than in cathedrals.

25

EACH OF US IS A TIME CAPSULE

Each of us is a living time capsule. The capsule is crammed with wistful memories of the tangibles and the intangibles of years past.

When we disclose the contents of our time capsule to the very young, twenty years in the future, they may react with incredulity. "What's this you said about posting letters in mail boxes, using wired telephones, snorting into linen hand-kerchiefs, and using carbon paper to make copies? Are you teasing?"

You may feel a sense of personal superannuation when you visit an antique shop and discover that many of these tangibles were new when you were a child or youth. If you are hesitant to reveal this to the youngsters with you, consider limiting your disclosures to memories that relate only to those intangibles that are not preserved physically and cannot be displayed in an antique shop or, worse, a museum. Mention the tradition of the Sunday family dinner, for example.

If you dare engage the doubt of your young companions, tell them about the fads of pet rocks, mood rings, and hula-hoops. Regale them with seeming fantasies, such as people who rinsed their gray-yellow hair with a subtle blue coloring to soften the contrast. Yes, children, older people with blue hair. Really!

Test your credibility with them further by recalling that college students at one time—mostly in 1939 and less so to 1970—swallowed live goldfish to demonstrate their daring. If they believe this, proceed to the next level of trust. Tell them about the propeller beanies worn by millions of children in the 1950s. Should they continue to believe such factual inanities, you deserve congratulations that your trustworthiness as a raconteur was not questioned.

You may want to tell them that today's adolescents are denied lasting educational benefits because of the declining availability of instructional gifts that did wonders to arouse engineering, architectural, and scientific interest among pre-teens. Lincoln Logs, model trains, Erector sets, chemistry sets and microscopes were sold in toy departments. These products were worth much more than mere entertainment value.

In our lives we have moments when we recall the pleasure of receiving company, perhaps in a living room that had a piano. We looked forward to television programs enjoyed by the entire family (Gun Smoke, Ed Sullivan, and many more), hearing someone whistle "a happy tune," swaying to the harmony of a barbershop quartet, redeeming books of S&H stamps, receiving the new Sears' mail catalog, and savoring ala-carte selections from a favored cafeteria where you could find foods not offered at home.

These and other comforts in life—including the home piano—have disappeared or are fading. What remains today as cultural artifacts may seem secure, but they too are likely to vanish except for memories of them in our "time capsules."

Store cashiers, paper receipts, incandescent bulbs, and election polling places are endangered because of electronic advancements. Freeways replaced by toll roads, the banning of boxing and football because of disabling injuries, stand-alone TV receivers replaced by multi-media laptops, Chinatowns without Chinese-Americans, and neighborhood taverns are all candidates for near-term extinction.

Obituaries for horse racing, jazz, opera, marriage, desktop computers, department stores, printed books, wired telephones, magazines, wrist watches and Saturday mail delivery have been drafted by daily newspapers for the proper moment of release.

Such things are—to borrow a phrase from Longfellow—"footprints on the sands of time." The sands are stored in our time capsules. We are the custodians of those footprints.

25

DOGS, CHILDREN OR NEITHER

David Brooks, columnist for the New York Times, wrote this comment in the November 18, 2012 edition: "The number of Americans who are living alone has shot up from 9 percent in 1950 to 28 percent today. In 1990, 65 percent of Americans said that children are very important to a successful marriage. Now, only 41 percent of Americans say they believe that. *There are now more American homes with dogs than with children* (emphasis added).

The concluding sentence of his comment should not be surprising. There are more American homes with dogs than with children because more households are able to have a dog than children. Age, choice, sterility, and financial constraints are some of the disqualifiers for parenthood.

The Brooks column might lead one to infer, incorrectly, that there are more dogs than children. The number of children, age 20 or under, is 87 million, based on Census Bureau data for 2010. The dog population, based on a survey of 50,000 pet owners conducted in 2011 by the American Veterinary Medical Association, is 70 million.

From 2006 through 2011 the number of children 20 years and younger increased 1 percent while, according to the aforementioned veterinary association, the number of pet dogs decreased by 3 percent. The Census Bureau projects the number of children will increase to 95 million in 2020 and 110 million by 2040.

The projected dog population is anyone's guess. A clue may be provided by a study cited by the Pet Food Industry, which showed a sharp drop in dog ownership among Americans age 55 to 64 "and an even sharper drop-off at the 65+ age level." As our population ages, there may be a continuing decline in the number of dogs relative to the number of children.

Who, or what, will do the most to promote more dogs as pets? Most likely, it will be the trend towards households having a single resident—those believed to be most in need of a dog's companionship. In 1940 only 7.7% of households were occupied by a single resident. The trend is moving steadily upward: 13.3% of households in 1960, 22.75% in 1980, 25.8% in 2000 and, in 2010, 28 percent.

Who, or what, will promote the types of dogs most popular with the American public? It will not be the movies or television shows featuring a lovable dog, such as Lassie

(1943-1973). Nor will it be a dog that belongs to a presidential First Family—they, too often, are rare breeds.

The Labrador retriever has held the top spot in the number of dog registrations since 1991. Rankings for the next 19 most popular dog types change moderately each year, with the number 2 spot currently (2012) held by the German shepherd.

Dogs residing in the White House do not influence breed selections by the public. Nor, apparently, do they influence demand for the number of dogs.

From John Adams, the first president to occupy the White House, to William McKinley, which represents all the presidents in the 1800s, half of the presidents had one or more dogs in the executive mansion.

Presidents have learned that having a dog endears them to a significant portion of the electorate. Yet they often select breeds with foreign origins. Presidents of the 20th century had these foreign breeds, among others: English bulldog (Harding), German shepherd (Coolidge), Irish wolfhound (Hoover), Scottish terrier (FDR and George W. Bush), Welsh Terrier (JFK), and Irish setter (Nixon).

Ronald Reagan and Barack Obama each trumped this list with more exotic selections: Reagan's Bouvier des Flandres Sheep Dog and Obama's Portuguese water dog. The latter two types failed to appear on the list of the American Kennel Club's 20-most popular dogs in 2012.

The popularity of "First Dogs" might increase if presidents select All-American breeds, such as the Boston terrier, American foxhound, American water spaniel, or the Chesapeake Bay retriever.

President John Tyler (1841-1845) strongly implied a preference for children to dogs. He had 8 children by his first wife, 7 by his second, and only one dog. The dog was a gift to his wife. Calvin Coolidge seemed to prefer dogs, of which he had twelve, but only two children. Being known as "Silent Cal," he never explained this imbalance. Tyler's imbalance requires no explanation.

American presidents, since 1963, have had a combined total of 20 children and 13 dogs. Obama has two children and one dog, George W. Bush had two children and two dogs, Clinton had one of each, George H.W. Bush had 6 children and 2 dogs, Carter had one dog, that, like Truman before him, he returned to the donor, and, again as with Truman, one child. Ford had 4 children and one dog. Nixon had two children and three dogs. Johnson had two of each.

One cannot say these latter-day presidents profoundly favored either children or dogs. Children have a slight edge in the competition, thanks to George H. W. Bush and Gerald Ford.

Which selection will dominate in the coming years: dogs, children, or neither? W. C. Fields (1879-1946), the sardonic comic and movie actor, held the view that the "neither" choice appealed to him. He said "anyone who hates children and dogs can't be all bad."

The happiest choice may be dogs and children. When one disappoints, you can seek solace from the other.

26

LIES—WHITE AND OTHER

Our lives would be more difficult if white lies were absolutely impermissible. "Honey," she asked coyly, "do these slacks make me look fat?" "Not at all," he replies, averting a harsh fate that would await an indiscreet, but truthful response. A waiter asks: "Is everything all right?" This is not a moment to interrupt the meal with a critique, unless the food has made the diner publicly nauseous or someone else's order was served.

Is there a Santa? Of course. An Easter bunny? You bet. A tooth fairy? Indeed! All three legends we certify as true when we choose not to disturb the pleasures of harmless, entertaining, fiction. At other times we seize the opportunity to establish credibility with children should they raise doubts about mythical events we find un-appealing. "No, George Washington did not chop down a cherry tree and St. Patrick did not drive all the snakes from Ireland." Get real!

Abraham Lincoln conducted himself with honesty. For him it was a practical matter. "Honest Abe" believed "no man has a good enough memory to make a successful liar." Did he never tell a white lie? Considering his wife's ill temper, Lincoln must have chosen his household words very carefully. That may have contributed to his skill in crafting the wording of his public addresses and documents.

Where are society's ethical boundaries for white lies? Is a sugar-pill placebo prescribed to relieve an imaginary ailment a physician's white lie, or is it compassion? Is wearing a Rolex watch known to be a counterfeit a white lie, or an ill-advised but subtle design endorsement? There can be, at the same moment, a blend of vice and virtue in our conduct.

At times the truth is muted or compromised to avoid unnecessary social un-pleasantries. Our vocabulary is rich with acceptable synonyms to avoid the use of the provocative word "lie"—exaggeration, rationalization, fib, and fish story are common examples. A serious untruth may more politely be termed as mendacity, a whopper, or a prevarication to avoid the inflammatory challenge of another's veracity.

If a harmless white lie is committed to achieve a higher-value purpose, is it immoral? Through the ages, eminent philosophers have held that telling a lie is never permissible. Immanuel Kant (1724-1804), a German philosopher who wrote on matters of ethics and other topics, Catholic ethicists St. Thomas Aquinas (1226-1274) and St. Augustine (354-430) all held that lying at any level is immoral.

Plato took a moderate view. He believed there are situations where lying is permissible if, for example, its intention is an act of compassion. "No, your cancer is not terminal."

Appraisal of the white lie as a matter of morality continues into modern times. Dan Ariely, a professor of psychology at Duke University, and author of The Honest Truth About Dishonesty (2012), told interviewer Brian Bethune of *Maclean's* magazine (7-23-12) that "we all need to lie a little bit to live in society."

Virginia Woolf made a stronger case for white lies when she had a character state, in her novel To The Lighthouse,: "To pursue truth with such astonishing lack of consideration for other people's feelings, to rend the thin veils of civilization so wantonly, so brutally, was to her so horrible an outrage of human decency…."

If modern ethics condones lying "a little bit" because it is seen as a necessity for the sake of "other people's feelings," exploiting this permissiveness can lead to slipping down the scale of truthfulness, descending into greyer and greyer shades of deceit.

Apparently most everyone is given an internal moral compass that defines how far we dare manipulate the truth. The *Daily Mail*, a United Kingdom newspaper, reported (3-30-10) that researchers at the Massachusetts Institute of Technology used a magnetic field generated "on a small part of the skull [creating] weak electric currents in the brain" where the moral compass lies, "just behind the right ear. By disrupting the brain's electric currents in this area, subjects were rendered temporarily less moral."

Experiences suggest to us that our moral navigation is innately guided, unless overpowered by one's willful vice. The moral compass, our conscience, sets boundaries. We may, for example, feel comfortable in taking home pencils from the office, but would not steal from a donation box even when the material gain is significant and the chance of exposure is nil. As civil beings we do not cross that moral boundary. We may tell a white lie, but never lie under oath.

Institutional behavior, driven by profit or power, lacks an innate moral compass. There are many recent examples. The manipulation of the London Inter-bank Offered Rate ("Libor"), the purpose of which is to establish a "self-regulated" interest rate, instead turned out to illegally benefit bank profits. Sub-prime high-risk home mortgages were bundled into securities and sold to unwary investors. Enron's "creative bookkeeping" brought ruin to the company and its long-established auditing firm, with a revered past (and no future), Arthur Andersen.

There was a time, in the 1920s and 1930s, authorities believed they could expose a lie by administering a dose of sodium pentothal, popularly called "the truth serum." If this barbiturate truly was effective, we could eliminate many audits simply by subjecting company executives to the truth-serum test. Sting operations—which are deceptions whereby police participate in illegal activities to gain the confidence of suspects—would be unnecessary. "Persons of interests" would be administered the truth serum and the police would avoid the dangers and humiliation of a failed sting.

By the 1950s scientists concluded that the truth serum was ineffective. It wasn't until 1963, however, that the U.S. Supreme Court declared the ingestion of a truth serum was unconstitutional and, thus, not admissible as evidence in court. The court left unanswered the issue of whether the drug works as claimed.

Polygraphs (lie-detector tests) also have been found inadmissible as evidence in court because they are viewed as scientifically unproven. Use of thermographic cameras to detect a rising temperature in the nose when one lies, as reported by *Science Daily* (12-4-12), is too new a development to be tested in a court case.

A bottle of wine may be an effective truth detector. It is probable that bartenders hear more honest testimony from semi-intoxicated patrons than judges hear from sworn defendants.

One potential derivative of lying may be self-deception, where we begin lying to our self. A diet soft drink is ordered with a bacon cheeseburger to deceive oneself into believing an off-setting caloric balance is achieved. Using euphemisms to rationalize a divorce—"we grew in different directions"—is more comforting than admitting "we lost interest in each other."

There is some reason to hope civil conduct is improving. The Josephson Institute of Ethics, a Los Angeles-based institution, surveyed 23,000 high-school students in 2012. The institute reported: "for the first time in a decade students are cheating, lying and stealing less than in previous years." The institute has conducted this type of national survey every two years since 1992. Their research is believed to indicate important trends on how students will act as adults.

Maybe our grandchildren will serve as role models to us.

27

SILVER LININGS ON OUR AGING SHADOW

October 1, 2012 was the "International Day of Older Persons." On that occasion several organizations, including some United Nation agencies, collaborated in a report entitled "Ageing in the Twenty-First Century: A Celebration and a Challenge."

That intriguing title provokes one to question: What is there to celebrate about aging, and what are the challenges? The report limited examination of celebration and challenge to a single perspective: "access to, and enjoyment of, the full range of human rights."

Let us look at a broader spectrum of challenges and the silver linings on the shadow of aging that we care to celebrate. Human rights, which we seniors generally enjoy as Americans, are left aside.

From our own personal experiences we can easily identify several physical, mental and social challenges commonly associated with aging, some of which worsen as age increases. What we recognize less easily is that most elderly

Americans are self-reliant, leading content and productive lives.

The American Psychological Association's report (April 1998), from its "Working Group on the Older Adult," states that only 9% of those between ages 65 and 69 need personal assistance, while up to 50% of those over 85 need assistance with everyday activities." The implication is that fewer than half of those over 85 may not need personal assistance.

The comforting data for those under 85 are supported in detail by the federal government's Administration on Aging in its report "A Profile of Older Americans—2011." The profile shows that for non-institutionalized elderly ages 65-74, 6% have difficulty bathing or showering, 5% have difficulty dressing, 2% eating, 9% getting in/out of bed, and 17% walking.

For those ages 75-84 the respective percentages are 14%, 10%, 4%, 15% and 28 percent. The statistical odds significantly favor the absence of such dependencies for those under the age of 85.

Before our celebration carries us too far, one should acknowledge the commonly-reported challenges of aging.

They include diminished hearing and vision, higher blood pressure, diabetes, a decrease in muscle mass and, on average by the age of 80, a loss of 2" in height and almost half of our sense of smell. For most of us, these are limitations with which we can function adequately, thanks to prescribed health products and services and to an increased capacity to cope with routine adversities.

Seniors 65 years of age and older apparently are more satisfied with their lives than those in the 50-64 age group. This is the conclusion of a survey asked of respondents, aged 50 years or older, in all 50 states, conducted in 2006 by the Center for Disease Control and Prevention in its study "The State of Mental Health and Aging in America: Life Satisfaction" (2006).

Nationally, 5.8% of respondents in the 50-64 age group said they were "dissatisfied" or "very dissatisfied" with their life. Only 3.5% of respondents among those 65 years or older said they were dissatisfied or very dissatisfied.

The two states having the highest percentages of dissatisfied or very dissatisfied respondents, among those 65 years or older, were California (4.7%) and New Jersey (4.6%). Hawaii (1.8%) and Iowa (2.1%) had the lowest percentages for this age group. In *every* state the 50-64 age group had higher percentages of those dissatisfied than the 65 or older group.

The elderly may have more health issues than those younger, but find more satisfaction with life. A United Kingdom publication, *The Telegraph* (8-7-09), cited research that "the elderly brain has the ability to let negative memories fade more quickly than the young." Other studies, reported by the same source, found that "older adults report less distress than other age groups … and emotional happiness improves with age."

It seems true, as John Webster wrote (Westward Hoe) in 1607, "Old wood does burn brighter."

28

TALK, TALK, TALK

The United States is increasingly a nation of many tongues. In 2009 80% of American households spoke only English at home, down from 86% in 1990. West Virginia in 2009 led the nation in homes where only English is spoken (98%), with California having the lowest percentage (57%).

Canada has tried to ameliorate its language differences. *Vive la difference?* Not in the Province of Quebec. French is its official language, treating all others as scarcely tolerable. Yankees visiting Quebec often complain that many Quebecers seem to comprehend when addressed in English, but re-act puzzled, as if they are monolingual.

Among those who speak only English in our country there often is a potential for mixed dialects, resulting in contrary interpretations. English has several family branches, among them Black English, the Queen's (or King's) English, American English, Southern English, Jive, and Rap. Then there are local accents found in Brooklyn, New England, and drawls in the "land of cotton." All are tinged with jargon and slang.

Henry Higgins, the phonetics professor in George Bernard Shaw's <u>Pygmalion</u> movie version, "My Fair Lady," was appalled by the linguistically-challenged Eliza Doolittle. The professor scolded her: "A woman who utters such depressing and disgusting sounds has no right to be anywhere—no right to live—don't sit there crooning like a bilious pigeon."

"Just you wait, Henry Higgins." Understanding each other in the United States may become more challenging than your transformation of Eliza.

English-speakers may temper inflammatory expressions by using gentler words. "Twit" is less offensive than calling someone a "jerk" or "nerd." Most of us are uncertain of the meaning of "twit" until we reach for a dictionary to find it is "a silly or foolish person." "Bilious" is not a common word, but then Henry Higgins vocabulary was not common, either.

Some four-letter words are acceptable in civil conversation. Others aren't. Crud, zany, drat, darn, geez, lewd, and dang are examples of four-letter words generally acceptable, probably because of their opaque meanings.

Shakespeare originated several dozen words when conventional vocabulary did not meet his needs. He is much acclaimed also for re-designing hundreds of existing words and idioms. That is not a practical option to those of us who are less creative. We do adapt, slowly, to new words that enter the standard lexicon each year.

Some words have an offensive coloring when used in an argumentative situation. Words like liberal, red-neck, bimbo, ding-bat, or gender-bender may seem benign to the speaker while hostile to a listener. Minorities complain others employ "code" words to disparage or identify them.

In 1942 a decision by the Supreme Court banned "fighting words [that] by their very utterance inflict injury or tend to incite an immediate breach of the peace," or have a "direct tendency to cause acts of violence by the person to whom, individually, the remark is addressed." Apparently that decision has yet to be applied to rowdy television audiences and belligerent sport fans.

Speech that hurts the feelings of a person does not reach the legal level of "fighting words," according to the Supreme Court. That provides a safe harbor to those who use e-mail and twitter to offend others without directly causing an act of violence. When one does not physically face an adversary, words tend to become braver, character more dissolute, and social norms ignored.

We hear that "silence is golden." Abraham Lincoln paid homage to that thought when he said: "Tis better to be silent and be thought a fool than to talk too much and remove all doubt." An anonymous wag observed: "It is seldom that God finds a soul quiet enough to speak to." The bible has the Creator ordering us to contemplative silence. "Be still, and know that I am God" (Psalm 46:10).

Who talks the most—men or women? In folklore it is believed women talk more than men. A study conducted by the University of Arizona, reported in *Science* magazine (7-6-07), refuted this popular myth by electronically "wiring" all conversations of 396 college students. The study found that women and men each utter about 16,000 words a day.

One would hope the most talkative people are educators, irrespective of gender.

29

WHY GOOD THINGS HAPPEN TO EVIL PEOPLE

In his popular book, <u>When Bad Things Happen to Good People</u> (1981), Rabbi Harold Kushner noted that the title is about "when," not "why." He explains that the purpose of the book is not to philosophize on *why*, but to help those who have been "hurt by life ... to find strength and hope."

This essay considers why good things happen to evil people, a question asked less often than why bad things happen to good people. The bible offers a brief answer: "Your Father, who is in heaven, makes His sun rise on the evil and the good, and sends rain on the righteous and unrighteous" (Matthew 5:45). Why is it that while it drizzles on the righteous, it often rains on the unrighteous?

The words *good* and *evil*, as used in this essay, need definition. Good here means illicit gain enjoyed through an illegal and/or immoral act. Evil describes the conduct of a person enriched by illicit gain that escapes just punishment.

The adjective "evil" is preferred to "bad." We all are a fusion of varying degrees of good and bad, with a minority of us truly evil. "There is so much good in the worst of us and so much bad in the best of us, that it hardly behooves any of us to talk about the rest of us," Kansas governor Hoch lyrically opined over a century ago. Politicians readily understand such ethical conundrums.

How can there be both good and evil if there is a Creator who teaches us love and justice? This question is the focus of the theological rationale called "Theodicy," which is a reasoned defense of God's goodness in view of the existence of evil. What are these defenses?

It begins with the doctrine of free will. As individuals we have choices of good or bad. We are guided by our conscience, but our will is free to make choices.

The Theory of Opposites is a complementary argument. We experience up and down, light and dark, hot and cold, rain and drought, famine and plenty, courage and fear and, yes, good and evil.

Can we conceive of good without experiencing evil? If one exists, the other exists, as do other paired opposites.

History has given us many examples of people who have reaped enrichments and power through evil deeds without suffering a consequential earthly penalty. Consider the tyrants that died natural deaths, including the infamous conquerors and plunderers Attila the Hun and Genghis Khan. Add Henry VIII, a homicidal oft-married husband, or Ivan the Terrible, a psychopath who died of a stroke while playing chess, or Josef Stalin, who executed millions, but died peacefully. Don't overlook the Kim dynasty that continues to rule North Korea.

There are examples other than tyrants that personify the presence of evil. Among them are hackers who steal electronically, those that exploit bankruptcy laws, health-care givers that defraud Medicare, corrupt politicians, and others. Many of these miscreants escape detection while they enjoy their ill-gotten gains.

Contrary to popular slogans, crime too often pays. Evil beckons when apprehension is unlikely. This is especially true of car thefts, house burglaries, stolen identities, and money laundering.

Solon, the lawmaker of ancient Greece, nicely summed up—perhaps too idealistically—the free-will choice made by good people: "Many evil men are rich, and good men poor, but we shall not exchange with them our excellence for riches."

30
DRIVING WHILE AGED

Police officers are not permitted to stop drivers on suspicions raised by racial profiling. The public is free, however, to question the driving skills of an elderly generation simply because of the age of its drivers. The imagined charge is: Driving While Aged.

Concern about the qualifications of the elderly driving may be related to the fact that those 65 years of age or older are an increasingly larger segment of the population. The stereotype of older drivers is that they threaten public safety. The inference drawn, therefore, is that our roads are becoming increasingly dangerous.

It's not that the highways currently are over-burdened with the number of aged drivers. The Federal Highway Administration (FHWA) reports that "79% of licensed drivers are between the ages of 20 and 64, 5% are under the age of 20, while [only] 16% are 65 years of age or older."

But times are changing. The specter of a generational "silver tsunami" looms ahead. "By the year 2030, one-fourth of American drivers will be 65 years of age or older," according to American Automobile Association's Foundation for Traffic Safety.

The FHWA adds that in 1990 66% of those ages 70 or older had a driver's license. By 2000 and 2009 the respective percentages grew to 70% and 84% of that age category.

Among younger age groups the opposite effect seems apparent, with a slightly lower percentage of the population licensed in each group in 2009 compared with 1990 and 2000.

Chronological age alone is not an adequate measure of one's driving ability. There are always those exceptional elderly stalwarts who are inspirational. Actor Paul Newman, at the age of 70, was the oldest driver to be a member of a winning team in a major race-car event. In 2005, at the age of 80, he participated in his last race.

In 2007 seventeen adventurers (65 years of age or older) motorcycled almost 700 miles, safely touring the island of Taiwan. Although some had motorcycle experience in past decades, none, immediately before the tour, had a current motorcycle license. The roads, often winding sharply, were unfamiliar to them.

Peter Starr, one of the bikers, reported "some of the riders had cancer or degenerative heart disease, and all of them suffered from arthritis" (*Motorcyclist* magazine, April 2012).

Among all adults, the decisive criterion for driving safely is one's health. The major issue is eyesight, followed by hearing, cognitive faculties, attentiveness, and reaction time.

Taking medications to manage a health problem can reduce one's driving alertness. Unfortunately, *not* taking prescribed medicines may also cause driving deficiencies.

Vehicle fatalities per 100,000 licensed drivers of all ages have fallen from 15 to 12 since 1975, thanks to seat belts, better roads and safer vehicles. Drivers in their sixties are said to drive as safely as those in their thirties.

Behind these comforting facts is the reality that "per-mile driven fatal crash rates increase starting at age 75 and increase markedly after age 80," according to the U.S. Department of Transportation's Fatality Analysis Reporting System. Octogenarians have 5.5 times as many fatal crashes per mile driven than do drivers in their middle ages.

What solutions might be available to enhance safe driving among elderly motorists? A couple of droll responses come to mind. One is to avoid left-turns, the cause of 28% of accidents involving older drivers. Another is to avoid driving in the day time, when 82% of such accidents occur.

Returning to a serious level, possible solutions include: designing safer cars marketed to the senior segment of auto buyers; enrolling in computer-assisted safe-driver training; having doctors report worrisome medical conditions to licensing authorities; encouraging self-policing among older drivers; and, requiring more-frequent eye testing among licensed drivers age 70 or older. Each possibility is considered briefly.

Although it sounds futuristic, self-driven automobiles are approaching reality. As of September 2012, Nevada, California and Florida permit self-driven cars on public roads if a human is inside to take over controls. Hawaii and Oklahoma are giving them serious consideration. They offer safety benefits to the general public, but particularly to teen-agers and the elderly.

Google has been a prime mover in promoting the technology, which they expect to see marketed in 2017. The company has its self-interest at stake, involving the ability to safely text and use cell phones while in self-driven vehicles. Toyota plans a "semi-autonomous" automobile designed primarily to assist elderly drivers.

Computer-assisted safe-driving training has been tested among Pennsylvania drivers by Allstate Insurance, using a program developed by Posit Science. The American Automobile Association has an on-line program, called Roadwise Review, "to help you identify steps to reduce risks in eight key areas…" Such programs help older drivers to periodically and safely assess their driving skills.

Requiring physicians to report to licensing agencies the identity of patients who need driving rehabilitation training, or suspension of their driving privileges, is a task the medical professions are not eager to pursue. Such requirements may prove counter-productive. Patients may avoid or prolong their visits with physicians. There is also the question of physician liability if a patient is involved in a serious accident.

Elderly drivers should be encouraged to police their own driving activities. Self-imposed restrictions commonly include not driving at night, avoiding unfamiliar roads, leaving a greater space between vehicles, and driving at or below the legal speed limit. Senior citizens are reluctant to stop using their automobiles, a treasured symbol of independent living.

Licensing requirements vary widely among states. There is insufficient research data to certify common standards nationwide. Simply requiring more-frequent testing of older drivers appears to some as age discrimination.

Yet 27 states, as of November 2012, have age-based requirements. Arizona, for example, issues a license which is valid until one reaches the age of 65, at which time renewing by mail must be accompanied by a vision-test conducted not more than 3 months prior to the re-application. Arizona drivers, age 70 or more, may not renew by mail.

Twenty-six other states have age-based license-renewal requirements. Renewals set by age vary broadly. The range begins with a low of 40 years (Maryland) and 50 years of age (Georgia)—both for vision tests. The upper range is 85 years of age (Texas), which mandates a 2-year license-renewal period instead of the 6-year renewal given to those under that age. More-frequent renewal periods typically begin at the age of 60 or 65 in states having age-based requirements.

Coming of age as seniors brings with it many benefits. Detracting from them, in coming years, may be the adoption of greater restrictions on driving privileges after the age of sixty-five.

31

THE RISE OF OUR WOMEN WARRIORS

This essay recounts our government's perceptions of women in combat, or women supporting combatants, from the American Revolutionary War to the January 2013 announcement by the Pentagon opening combat roles to women.

The 13 colonies that preceded formation of the United States each required able-bodied white men to join their respective citizens' militia. During our War of Independence colonies, on occasion, would draft men when there were insufficient numbers of militia volunteers. The first national draft did not occur until the Civil War, when both sides adopted their separate, but ineffectual, draft systems.

The "Selective Service System," authorized by the congress in 1940, was suspended in 1973. The nation then depended on an all-volunteer military. Males between the ages of 18 and 25 were required to continue to register in the event inductions had to be re-activated.

Only males were required to register. President Carter, in 1980, tried to persuade congress to revise the Selective Service System to include women. Congress balked.

That led to litigation the following year, in which the Supreme Court was asked to decide if the male-only policy was gender discrimination in violation of the Fifth Amendment. In *Rostker v. Goldberg* the court decided 6 to 3 that the Selective Service System did not violate the due-process clause of the Constitution.

The majority opinion of the court stated: "Since women are excluded from combat service by statute or military policy, men and women are simply not similarly situated for purposes of a draft or registration for a draft..." President Carter believed women should be drafted for non-combatant positions. The court held that "the need for non-combat roles during mobilization can be met by volunteers."

If the Supreme Court has ruled that women are immune from the draft because the purpose of the Selective Service System is to induct male citizens for possible combat roles, is it not reasonable to assume that women should be draft-eligible when combat roles are officially opened to them? As long as we have an all-volunteer military, this question is muted. What happens when we run short of volunteers and the Selective Service System is re-activated? Congress will have to decide.

General George Washington had to tolerate women camp followers during the War of Independence because many were married to soldiers. Driving off the women would have encouraged some husbands to desert. Women did provide essential services needed by the army, but feeding the women and, at the same time, mobilizing fighting forces created problems.

Washington wrote (August 4, 1777): "the multitude of women … are a clog upon every movement." He urged his officers to "get rid of all such as are not absolutely necessary." A few women disguised themselves as men to fight in the revolution.

In the War of 1812 Lucy Brewer, disguised as a male, became the first woman Marine. She served as a combatant aboard the USS Constitution ("Old Ironsides"). The Marine Corp did not actively recruit women until August 1918.

During the Civil War, neither side deliberately enlisted women. A few hundred women are believed to have dressed as men in order to serve as combatants. Without physical examinations of recruits, infrequent bathing, and the enrollment of many under-aged barely-masculine males, it was difficult to determine the gender of some enlistees simply by their outer appearance.

Dr. Mary Edwards Walker, the first female surgeon to serve the U.S. Army, treated Union soldiers and civilians during the Civil War. She is the only woman awarded the Congressional Medal of Honor.

Physical examinations of recruits began in the Spanish-American War (1898). Certified nurses were hired as non-military personnel, dispensing with the practice of relying on free-lance medics.

Nurses serving without military status continued as a policy in World War I. Some 21,000 nurses volunteered. Another 11,000 women served in the Navy, mostly in clerical positions, but without training or military recognition.

World War II broadened military involvement for women, during which 350,000 women served in or with the U.S. Armed Forces. The Women Airforce Service Pilots (WASP) flew every type of military aircraft from their factories of origin to military bases. WASP also transported troops and cargo. Considered civil servants during the war, it took 32 years after the war before the WASP were given military-veteran status.

The 83,000 uniformed Navy WAVES of World War II (Women Accepted for Voluntary Emergency Service) fared better. They earned the same pay as men and shared with men many non-combatant assignments. Mildred McAfee, the founding director of the WAVES, was the first woman commissioned as an officer in the Naval Reserve. At the conclusion of the war, the WAVES program was disbanded.

The Army's WACS (Women's Army Corp) enrolled over 150,000 women during World War II. In 1978 the WACS program also was disbanded.

President Truman opened military enlistments for women in 1948 by signing the Women's Armed Services Integration Act. This act did little to fully integrate women into the military. Their number was capped at 2% of the armed-forces personnel. They were denied the top ranks of service and prohibited from combat. The 2% ceiling was repealed in 1967.

In 1971 the first woman was promoted to brigadier general, the Air Force's Jeanne M. Holm. In 2008 Ann E. Dunwoody became the first woman to be named a four-star general. As of November 2012 the U.S. military had 64 women generals on active duty.

Among all service branches, approximately 22,000 women served during the Korean War. One-third provided medical services and, of these, 600 served in combat zones. During the 1950s the percentage of women as a total of the armed forces declined, the result of fewer women volunteering, a reduced recruiting effort, and unequal promotion opportunities.

In the Vietnam War, 10,000 women served in or near Vietnam, a small percentage of the 250,000 women who were in service at some time during our long military involvement in that conflict. Among the 10,000 were 6,250 nurses.

The First Gulf War (1990-91) deployed 40,000 American military women to that theatre, together with 500,000 American military men. Fifteen of these women were killed and two were taken prisoner by Iraqi soldiers.

Women pilots in that war were authorized, for the first time, to engage in combat. A woman pilot led a group of Chinook helicopters on the first day of the ground war. Helicopters piloted by women transported troops over enemy lines.

Although women soldiers were officially prohibited from engaging in direct ground combat in Iraq during the Second Gulf War, their presence in combat zones resulted in over 100 of them killed and many more wounded. If the enemy was unexpectedly engaged, women fought alongside their male comrades.

In the Second Gulf War and in Afghanistan, women Marines were assigned to combat units to pat-down ("frisk") females to search for hidden weapons and explosives. Known as "lionesses," this assignment could only be carried out by women.

Women in our military are increasingly exposed to direct-combat by insurgents. The conventional "front lines" and "rear lines" of past wars no longer exist. Combat can occur anywhere and everywhere. Rules made to shield women from combat no longer are defensible.

Should women be assigned to direct combat positions? The Pentagon's announcement of January 24, 2013, lifting a 1994 ban on women combatants, reflects the realities of modern war. The armed forces have until January 2016 to implement this policy or indicate special exceptions excluding women from specified military positions and assignments.

As of January 2013 the conflicts in Iraq and Afghanistan incurred 152 female troops killed and over 860 wounded. Approximately 250,000 women—10% of the total U.S. military personnel deployed in these conflicts—served in either of these two theatres over the years.

If women are to be assigned to conflicts where there are no delineated combat zones, they should be trained to defend themselves. Women today constitute 14% of the active-duty army and 20% of new recruits. We are increasingly dependent on them to serve, recognizing that most of them are not expected to volunteer for combat.

Eighty-three reference sources were reviewed to research this essay. Readers who wish to have a source identified for any particular segment may contact waltsonneville@verizon.net

32

IS EVERYBODY HAPPY

Ted Lewis, a well-known bandleader during the 1920s and into the 1960s, had a signature phrase: "Is evvvvvverybody happy?" He stretched the word "everybody" to emphasize *every*body.

His rhetorical question expected no response. What if the question was raised to you with a response expected. How would you reply?

Professionals who research happiness generally believe our happiest years are the age of innocence prior to our teens and the time following entry into our senior years. The middle years—somewhere in our 40's—are the most stressful, characterized in some cases by a "mid-life crisis."

Why would we be happier in our senior years? Julie Klam, writing in *Redbook* magazine (October 2012), had these tongue-in-cheek reasons why women might appreciate their senior years: you don't have to worry about getting pregnant; no kids in elementary school; you are eligible for senior discounts; you make your own rules; and, you do not have to be agreeable just to be polite.

Klam's last two points, on rules and acting polite, were practiced by two famous personalities: Albert Einstein and Emily Dickenson. Both were happy and both were eccentric. Einstein made his own rule after promising his doctor that he would no longer purchase tobacco. That led him to pick up cigarette butts off the street to smoke the salvaged tobacco in his pipe. Miss Dickenson seldom left her home and would not receive visitors. Rather impolite of her, but she was happy.

It does not seem advisable to become eccentric in your search for happiness unless you have gained public adulation for a laudable achievement.

Our happiest years may have been the era when our favorite entertainers performed. Or a time of cultural transition, such as the 1960s. Maybe it was a time when your debilitated health returned to normal, or when serenity was found in religion, or when your home became a tranquil "empty nest" as the children moved out.

Several studies indicate that raising children typically does not increase the happiness level of the parents. "The broad message is not that children make you less happy; it's just that children don't make you more happy," according to behavioral economist Andrew Oswald, who surveyed tens of thousands of Britons who were parents or non-parents.

Our gateway to happiness sometimes begins with a move to a more agreeable location. *Forbes* magazine (1-9-13) produced a list of the happiest cities "to work in right now." Dayton OH, Knoxville TN, Honolulu HI, Memphis TN, and Pittsburgh PA were the top five, according to their reported poll of 36,000 employees.

For the general population (workers and others), *Success* magazine (5-8-12) found the top five happiest cities were Arlington VA, Sioux Falls SD, Madison WI, Durham NC, and St. Paul/Minneapolis. If you are desperate to uplift your disposition, a move to any of these locations may change your happiness quotient.

Some find happiness based simply on the season of the year. The drama of a severe snow storm may bring excitement not matched by a trip to the beach. Snow-flocked trees and wind-sculpted snow drifts often produce remarkably artistic landscapes to bring you the delights of winter.

Darkness stimulates the amount of melatonin our body produces, a hormone that makes one sleepy. If you like to nap and sleep, winter's gloom may bring you happiness, although it is hard to imagine anyone wishing you a dark-and-gloomy holiday season.

Spring and summer can enrich a sense of wellbeing if one craves fresh fruits and vegetables. Oppressive heat, drought and floods can trigger a despair that quickly vanquishes the pleasure of farm and orchard products.

Our happiest memories may have been borne of not-so-happy times. Parents that require their children to take music lessons, or badger them to play golf or tennis, can encounter grudging resistance. Years later these disciplines could be sources of enjoyment and status for those who mastered their childhood lessons.

Trying to forecast what will make us happy in the future has all the certainty of crystal-ball gazing. We anticipate our future wants through whom and what we are today. Ask the law-school graduates that decide to become chefs or landscapers, or divorced people that elect to live alone, or ex-priests who marry, ask them if forecasting one's future wants is reliable.

Thomas Jefferson wisely implied in the Declaration of Independence that we are not assured of happiness. We have only the unalienable right to the pursuit of happiness.

Expectations of happy days sometimes are illusionary. It may happen that the happiest day was not when you bought a motor-home or motor-boat. It was the day you sold those items. The best time of marriage was not the honeymoon to which you looked forward. It was the many years you appreciate your spouse as a companion, provider, cook or nurse.

A greatly elevated income rarely brings happiness. A study released in 2010 by two Princeton professors, economist Daniel Kahneman and psychologist Angus Deaton, indicates that for Americans this is true only until annual income reaches a relatively-modest level of $75,000. Then the level of happiness plateaus.

Multi-billionaire Warren Buffett's life style has changed little, despite his enormous wealth. He lives in the same five-bedroom house he bought in 1958 and is said, at the age of 82, to prefer the luncheon items he has selected frequently over his many years: a hamburger with fries, followed by vanilla ice cream. While his fortune continues to aggregate, his happiness quotient appears unchanged over the decades.

Mr. Buffett might appreciate an observation made by an audience member of the televised Phil Donahue Show, some

25 years ago. The guest offered this simple formula for happiness, telling an inquiring Donahue: "All a man needs to be happy is a little red pickup truck, his own cement mixer, and a Chinese bride." Lottery players, with dreams of megabucks, would not understand this homespun philosophy.

Some governmental bodies are trying to determine if their citizens are happy. Nations periodically measure and announce their "Gross National Product" (GNP), which is the annual monetary sum of the country's goods and services. Why not measure something more meaningful, specifically an index of "Gross National Happiness" (GNH)?

A GNH initiative was launched in the tiny Himalayan Kingdom of Bhutan in 1972, with the help of two Canadian researchers. The initiative subsequently was adopted by the cities of Seattle, Eau Claire, Victoria British Columbia, and Decorah a small town in Iowa. Brazil, Canada, and France are said to be considering similar initiatives. The United Kingdom in 2012 said it would begin releasing a "Happiness Index" with its quarterly reports on Gross National Product.

The need for a Happiness Index was anticipated by the British economist Sir William Henry Beveridge (1879-1963). He observed that "the object of government, in peace and in war, is not the glory of the rulers or the races, but the happiness of the common man."

33

DON'T EXPECT THIS TO HAPPEN

Some things in life are never expected to happen. The sun setting in the east is an obvious example.

We are certain some events will never happen, for example opera fans creating a riot. Booing and hissing—yes, but rioting, never!

Shockingly, it did happen May 10, 1849 at the Astor Opera House in New York City. At least 22 people were killed and 142 injured over a dispute between opposing fans of two actors.

Can a "Dream Team" of professional basketball players lose to college players? Never! Incredibly, that too happened when the professional players lost in a scrimmage game to college players in La Jolla, CA in 1992, by a humiliating score of 62 to 54.

That Dream Team, however, went on to win the next scrimmage against the same collegians, later regaining their pride when they won in the Barcelona Olympics Summer Games that same year.

There are many events in life we never expect to happen. Chicago baseball fans may have less confidence in the Cubs winning a World Series than in an asteroid catastrophically slamming into the Wrigley Building.

Those weight-loss pills advertised on television—the ones that are "not available in stores"—may drain water from your body, but don't expect a lasting weight loss.

It is always safe to buy a Washington Redskins jersey. The chance of the team changing its name, in deference to those who find the name "Redskins" objectionable, is zero. The brand, unlike its critics, has a vested market value.

Don't expect this year's flu shot to protect you from a new strain that is circulating. Flu bugs know how to survive through mutations unexpected by our medical scientists.

Comic strips, on which you depended for years for a daily smile, can't be expected to continue to amuse. Most of them are wispy vestiges of the creations of their original artists.

New hit-songs can't be expected to be composed if advertisement agencies can't find the talent to create simple, amusing jingles for their client's products. "Golden Oldies" are revived to satisfy their needs.

No one expects nature to love a vacuum. For eons we have seen that nature really does abhor a vacuum. There are many households where this can be demonstrated.

Some day Christmas will arrive and Bing Crosby will not be heard singing "White Christmas." It could happen the year you find in your gift exchange something you actually want. Be patient. We have seen that the greatly unexpected can happen.

CONTENTS OF TWO OTHER BOOKS OF ESSAYS BY WALT SONNEVILLE

Contents of <u>My Twenty-Two Cents Worth</u>

Corrupting the English Language
Is the Earth the Universe's Insane Asylum
Our Fears Can Imprison or Isolate Us

Our Best and Worst Presidents
Do Public Libraries Have a Future
The Four Seasons of our Lives

Free Will or Pre-Disposition
Mother Nature and Her Children
Disappointments: We Have a Few

Are Dogs People
Love and Marriage, or Marriage and Love
What is Heaven Like

Appreciated and Unappreciated Inventions
Citizenship Tests: Can You Pass One
Getting Older but not Old

Is the United States a Christian Nation
Sleep and Humor
Religions' Common Values and War

Retirement Postponed or Avoided
Personal Security and Senior Citizens
Selecting the Greatest Generation

Obituaries Can Inform and Inspire
Banish Banal Expressions
Pet Peeves Follow Us Around

Yesteryears' Irreplaceable Songwriters
Assessing our Friendships
Romancing the Pirates No More

Life's Forty-Two Million Minutes
When Zero Tolerance Becomes Intolerable
Post-closures: Yesteryears' Lost Pleasures

Selecting a Favorite Philosopher
Our Nation's Changes
Mankind's Next Evolution

Contents of A Musing Moment

Grand- Parenting: Agonies & Ecstasies
Should Seniors Get Discounts
Should Seniors Retire to Help the Young

Is the Only-Child Trend Desirable
Balancing Self Doubt
Mourning the Deceased

Cemeteries and Their Alternatives
Reincarnation: What's Your Wish
Consistencies in Our Interesting Times

Taboos in the Land of the Free
When Weekdays were Dedicated
The Most-Impressive Movie Actress

Dating in Years of Yore
We Need a Hall of Shame
The Age of Post-Fraternalism

What We Owe Native Americans
Lawns: Rhymes with Yawns
Is Moonshine Liquor Returning

Court-Appointed Lawyers for Pets
What's in Your Medicine Cabinet
Inspiration from the Afflicted

Editing Our Given Names
The Wise Don't Prophesize
Doing Without a College Degree

Do You Collect, Clutter, or Hoard
History's Most Influential Person
Reconsidering the Seven Deadly Sins

Using and Losing Our Mind
The Decline of Legislated Morality
Question Famous Quotations

Our Words Retire Too
Twin Destinies: The Auto and Ourselves
Reflections on Seniors and Wine

———————

www.ingramcontent.com/pod-product-compliance
Lightning Source LLC
Chambersburg PA
CBHW061642040426
42446CB00010B/1546